Type 2 Diabetes Cookbook for Beginners

2000+ Days of Nutritious, Flavorful, and Low Sugar Recipes to Help You Manage Your Blood Sugar without Giving Up Your Favorite Meals 60 Days Meal Plan Included

Sienna Gracelyn

Table of Contents

Discover Your Exclusive Free Bonus!

Thank you for choosing "Type 2 Diabetes Cookbook for Beginners! We are excited to support your journey towards better health and wellness with three exclusive free bonus.

Scan the QR code to download these valuable resources:

Bonus 1: Mediterranean Diet Cookbook for Beginners
Enjoy another great book from the same author, focusing on the Mediterranean diet and its health benefits.

Bonus 2: Diabetes-Friendly Grocery List
A comprehensive list of diabetes-friendly foods to simplify your shopping trips and make meal planning easier.

Bonus 3: Beginner's Exercise Guide for Diabetes Management
A guide with easy-to-follow exercise routines for beginners, including walking, stretching, and basic strength training exercises.

Don't miss out on these incredible bonus! Scan the QR code to download your free resources and continue your journey towards managing your diabetes with delicious meals and effective exercise. Happy reading and good health!

Introduction

Welcome to Your Journey to Health

Welcome! You've taken an important step towards improving your health and managing type 2 diabetes through the power of nutrition. Whether you're newly diagnosed or looking to refine your dietary habits, this book is designed to guide you with supportive and practical advice. Living with diabetes can be challenging, but with the right tools and knowledge, you can take control and thrive.

Understanding the Importance of Diet in Managing Diabetes

The role of diet in managing diabetes cannot be overstated. Food is not just sustenance; it's a key player in how your body functions and how effectively you can manage your blood sugar levels. By choosing the right foods, you can help stabilize your blood sugar, reduce the risk of complications, and improve your overall well-being.

Type 2 diabetes is often described as a lifestyle disease, which means that lifestyle changes can have a profound impact on its management. One of the most significant lifestyle changes you can make is adopting a diet that supports your health needs. This doesn't mean you have to give up all the foods you love or start eating things you dislike. It's about finding a balance and making informed choices that align with your health goals.

How to Use This Book

This book is divided into two main sections. The first section provides a comprehensive understanding of type 2 diabetes, covering everything from the basics of the disease to debunking common myths. This foundation will help you understand why certain foods and habits are recommended, empowering you to make informed decisions.

The second section is filled with delicious, diabetes-friendly recipes. These recipes are designed to be easy to prepare, affordable, and enjoyable. Whether you're cooking for yourself, your family, or hosting a gathering, you'll find a variety of meals that cater to different tastes and dietary preferences.

Each recipe comes with detailed instructions, nutritional information, and tips to help you make the most of your culinary experience. We've also included meal plans and shopping lists to make your journey even smoother.

Having these tools on hand will not only make cooking easier but also more enjoyable. It sets the stage for you to explore and experiment with the recipes provided.

Reflecting on Your Journey

As you embark on this journey, it's important to reflect on your motivations and goals. Why do you want to manage your diabetes? What are your long-term health goals? Taking the time to answer these questions can provide clarity and direction.

Set Realistic Goals: Start with small, achievable goals. This could be something as simple as incorporating more vegetables into your meals or walking for 30 minutes a day. Celebrate your progress along the way, no matter how small it may seem.

Stay Motivated: Keeping your motivation high can be challenging, but it's essential for long-term success. Find what inspires you, whether it's reading success stories, setting rewards for yourself, or visualizing your future healthy self.

Embrace Change: Change can be difficult, but it's also an opportunity for growth. Embrace the changes you're making as positive steps towards a healthier life. Be patient with yourself and recognize that setbacks are a natural part of the process.

Final Encouragement

Managing type 2 diabetes through diet and lifestyle changes is a powerful way to take control of your health. It's a journey that requires commitment, but the rewards are well worth it. Improved energy levels, better blood sugar control, and a reduced risk of complications are just a few of the benefits you can look forward to.

This book is here to support you every step of the way. Use it as a resource, a guide, and a source of inspiration. Remember, you have the power to make positive changes and live a healthy, fulfilling life.

Thank you for choosing this book as your guide. Here's to your journey towards better health and well-being. Let's get started!

Section One: Understanding Type 2 Diabetes

Chapter 1: What is Diabetes?

The Basics of Diabetes

Diabetes is a chronic condition where your body struggles to regulate blood sugar levels. Normally, food is broken down into glucose, which enters your bloodstream. Insulin, a hormone produced by the pancreas, helps glucose enter your cells for energy. In diabetes, either the body doesn't make enough insulin or can't use it effectively, leading to high blood sugar levels. Persistent high blood sugar can cause severe health problems such as heart disease, vision loss, and kidney disease.

Type 1 vs. Type 2 Diabetes
Type 1 Diabetes:

Type 1 diabetes is an autoimmune disease where the immune system attacks insulin-producing beta cells in the pancreas. This condition often starts in childhood or adolescence but can develop at any age. Genetic and environmental factors contribute to this disease. People with type 1 diabetes need daily insulin injections or an insulin pump to survive.

- **Key Points:**
    - **Onset:** Often sudden and severe, typically in youth.
    - **Symptoms:** Increased thirst, frequent urination, extreme hunger, unintended weight loss, fatigue, blurred vision.
    - **Management:** Requires insulin therapy, blood sugar monitoring, diet, and exercise.

Type 2 Diabetes:

Type 2 diabetes is more common and typically develops in adulthood, though it is increasingly diagnosed in children and teens. This form of diabetes arises from insulin resistance and inadequate insulin production. Lifestyle factors like obesity, inactivity, and poor diet, along with genetic predispositions, significantly contribute to type 2 diabetes.

- **Key Points:**
    - **Onset:** Gradual, often asymptomatic initially.
    - **Symptoms:** Increased thirst, frequent urination, increased hunger, fatigue, blurred vision, slow-healing sores, frequent infections.
    - **Management:** Lifestyle changes (diet, exercise), oral medications, insulin in some cases.

Understanding the differences between type 1 and type 2 diabetes is crucial for proper management and treatment.

Symptoms and Diagnosis
Common Symptoms:

Recognizing symptoms is the first step toward diagnosis and management:

- **Increased Thirst and Frequent Urination:** High blood sugar pulls fluid from tissues, causing thirst and frequent urination.
- **Extreme Hunger:** Energy-deprived cells trigger intense hunger.
- **Unintended Weight Loss:** Despite eating more, weight loss occurs as the body uses fat and muscle for energy.
- **Fatigue:** Deprived cells lead to tiredness and irritability.
- **Blurred Vision:** High blood sugar affects the lenses in your eyes.
- **Slow-Healing Sores and Frequent Infections:** Diabetes hampers healing and infection resistance.
- **Areas of Darkened Skin:** Dark, velvety skin patches often indicate insulin resistance.

Diagnosis:

Diagnosing diabetes involves blood tests:
- **Fasting Plasma Glucose (FPG) Test:** Measures blood sugar after fasting overnight. Levels of 126 mg/dL or higher on two tests indicate diabetes.
- **A1C Test:** Shows average blood sugar over the past 2-3 months. An A1C level of 6.5% or higher on two tests indicates diabetes.
- **Oral Glucose Tolerance Test (OGTT):** Measures blood sugar before and after drinking a sweet liquid. Levels of 200 mg/dL or higher 2 hours post-drink indicate diabetes.
- **Random Blood Sugar Test:** High levels (200 mg/dL or higher) at any time, regardless of the last meal, indicate diabetes.

Early diagnosis and treatment can prevent complications and improve health.

Risk Factors

Knowing the risk factors helps in prevention and early detection.

Type 1 Diabetes Risk Factors:
- **Family History:** Having a relative with type 1 diabetes.
- **Genetics:** Certain genes increase risk.
- **Geography:** Higher incidence in certain countries.
- **Age:** Commonly diagnosed in children and adolescents.

Type 2 Diabetes Risk Factors:
- **Weight:** Overweight individuals are at higher risk.
- **Inactivity:** Lack of physical activity leads to insulin resistance.
- **Family History:** Relatives with type 2 diabetes increase your risk.
- **Age:** Risk increases after age 45.
- **Gestational Diabetes:** History of gestational diabetes raises risk.
- **High Blood Pressure:** Often linked with type 2 diabetes.
- **Cholesterol Levels:** Low HDL and high triglycerides increase risk.

Other Risk Factors:
- **Polycystic Ovary Syndrome (PCOS):** Women with PCOS are at higher risk.

- **Race/Ethnicity:** Higher prevalence among African Americans, Hispanics, Native Americans, and Asian Americans.

Long-term Complications

Diabetes can lead to various complications, especially if blood sugar levels are not well-controlled. These complications highlight the importance of effective management:

Cardiovascular Disease:

Diabetes increases the risk of heart disease, heart attack, stroke, and atherosclerosis. Managing blood sugar, blood pressure, and cholesterol can reduce this risk.

Nerve Damage (Neuropathy):

High blood sugar can damage nerves, particularly in the legs, causing tingling, numbness, and pain. Severe cases may result in loss of sensation in the affected limbs.

Kidney Damage (Nephropathy):

Diabetes can damage the kidneys' filtering system, leading to kidney failure or end-stage kidney disease, requiring dialysis or a kidney transplant.

Eye Damage (Retinopathy):

Diabetes can damage retinal blood vessels, potentially causing blindness. It also increases the risk of cataracts and glaucoma.

Foot Damage:

Poor blood flow and nerve damage increase the risk of foot complications. Untreated cuts and blisters can lead to serious infections and may require amputation.

Skin Conditions:

Diabetes increases susceptibility to bacterial and fungal infections.

Hearing Impairment:

Hearing problems are more common in people with diabetes.

Alzheimer's Disease:

Type 2 diabetes may increase the risk of dementia, including Alzheimer's disease. Poor blood sugar control appears to heighten this risk.

Final Thoughts

Understanding diabetes, recognizing symptoms, and knowing the risk factors are essential steps in managing the disease effectively. Early diagnosis and proper management can significantly reduce the risk of complications and enhance your quality of life.

This book aims to equip you with the knowledge and tools to take control of your diabetes through informed dietary choices and lifestyle changes. With determination, support, and the right information, you can manage your diabetes and live a healthy, fulfilling life. Let's embark on this journey together towards better health.

Chapter 2: Managing Diabetes with Diet

The Impact of Food on Blood Sugar

Managing diabetes effectively requires a comprehensive understanding of how different foods impact blood sugar levels. Every meal you eat can either help you maintain stable blood sugar levels or cause them to spike and crash. Understanding these impacts is crucial for making informed dietary choices.

When you consume food, your body breaks it down into glucose, which enters your bloodstream. The speed and extent to which food raises your blood sugar depend on several factors, including the type of food, portion size, and your body's insulin response. Foods high in carbohydrates typically have the most significant impact on blood sugar levels.

To manage diabetes, it's essential to focus on foods that provide steady energy without causing dramatic spikes in blood sugar. This includes understanding the types of carbohydrates, the role of protein and fat, the importance of fiber, and the timing of your meals.

Carbohydrates and Glycemic Index
Understanding Carbohydrates:

Carbohydrates are the body's primary source of energy. They are found in foods such as bread, rice, pasta, fruits, vegetables, and dairy products. When you eat carbohydrates, your body breaks them down into glucose, which enters your bloodstream.

There are three main types of carbohydrates:
- **Sugars:** Simple carbohydrates found in fruits, vegetables, milk, and sweeteners.
- **Starches:** Complex carbohydrates found in grains, legumes, and starchy vegetables.
- **Fiber:** A type of carbohydrate that the body cannot digest, found in fruits, vegetables, whole grains, and legumes.

Glycemic Index (GI):

The Glycemic Index is a ranking of carbohydrates on a scale from 0 to 100 based on how quickly and how much they raise blood sugar levels after eating. Foods with a high GI are rapidly digested and cause significant spikes in blood sugar levels, while foods with a low GI are digested more slowly and cause gradual increases in blood sugar levels.
- **High GI Foods (70 and above):** White bread, white rice, sugary drinks, and snacks.
- **Medium GI Foods (56-69):** Whole wheat products, brown rice, sweet potatoes.
- **Low GI Foods (55 and below):** Most fruits, vegetables, legumes, and whole grains.

Choosing low GI foods can help you manage your blood sugar levels more effectively. Incorporating more low GI foods into your diet means your body gets a steady supply of energy, which helps in maintaining stable blood sugar levels throughout the day.

Protein and Fat Considerations
Role of Protein:

Protein is essential for building and repairing tissues and is a crucial component of every cell in your body. Unlike carbohydrates, protein has a minimal effect on blood sugar levels, making it an important part of a diabetes-friendly diet. Including adequate protein in your meals can help you feel full and satisfied, reducing the likelihood of overeating.

Good sources of protein include:
- Lean meats (chicken, turkey, lean beef)
- Fish and seafood
- Eggs
- Dairy products (milk, cheese, yogurt)
- Plant-based proteins (beans, lentils, tofu, tempeh, nuts, and seeds)

Role of Fat:

Fats are a concentrated source of energy and play several vital roles in the body, including supporting cell growth, protecting organs, and aiding in nutrient absorption. However, not all fats are created equal. It's important to focus on healthy fats while limiting unhealthy fats.

- **Healthy Fats:** Unsaturated fats, which can help reduce inflammation and improve heart health. Sources include avocados, nuts, seeds, olive oil, and fatty fish like salmon.

- **Unhealthy Fats:** Saturated and trans fats, which can increase the risk of heart disease and worsen insulin resistance. Sources include fried foods, processed snacks, and fatty cuts of meat.

Balancing protein and healthy fats in your diet can help stabilize blood sugar levels and support overall health. Including these macronutrients in your meals can slow down the absorption of carbohydrates, leading to more gradual increases in blood sugar.

The Importance of Fiber

Fiber is a type of carbohydrate that the body cannot digest. It passes through the digestive system relatively intact, aiding in digestion and helping to regulate blood sugar levels. There are two types of fiber: soluble and insoluble.
- **Soluble Fiber:** Dissolves in water to form a gel-like substance, helping to lower blood glucose and cholesterol levels. Good sources include oats, fruits, vegetables, and legumes.
- **Insoluble Fiber:** Does not dissolve in water and helps add bulk to the stool, aiding in regular bowel movements. Good sources include whole grains, nuts, seeds, and vegetables.

Fiber has several benefits for people with diabetes:
- **Slows Digestion:** Helps slow the absorption of sugar, preventing spikes in blood sugar levels.
- **Increases Satiety:** Promotes a feeling of fullness, which can help control appetite and reduce overeating.
- **Improves Heart Health:** Can help lower cholesterol levels and reduce the risk of heart disease.

Aim to include a variety of fiber-rich foods in your diet. The recommended daily intake of fiber is about 25 grams for women and 38 grams for men, though most people fall short of these amounts.

Meal Timing and Frequency

When you eat can be just as important as what you eat. Spacing your meals and snacks throughout the day can help maintain stable blood sugar levels and prevent extreme highs and lows.

Regular Meal Schedule:

Establishing a regular meal schedule helps keep your blood sugar levels steady. This typically includes three main meals and one to three snacks spaced evenly throughout the day. Eating at consistent times helps your body regulate blood sugar more effectively and can prevent overeating.

Balanced Meals:

Each meal should contain a balance of carbohydrates, protein, and healthy fats. This combination helps slow the absorption of glucose into the bloodstream and provides sustained energy. For example, a balanced breakfast might include whole grain toast (carbohydrates), an egg (protein), and avocado slices (healthy fat).

Portion Control:

Managing portion sizes is crucial for controlling blood sugar levels. Overeating can lead to large spikes in blood sugar, while eating too little can cause it to drop. Using smaller plates, measuring portions, and being mindful of hunger cues can help you eat the right amount.

Smart Snacking:

Healthy snacks can help keep your blood sugar levels stable between meals. Opt for snacks that combine protein, fiber, and healthy fats, such as a small handful of nuts, a piece of fruit with cheese, or vegetable sticks with hummus.

Listening to Your Body:

Pay attention to how your body responds to different foods and meal timings. Everyone's body is different, so it's essential to find a routine that works best for you. Keeping a food diary can help you track what you eat, how much you eat, and how your blood sugar responds.

Conclusion

Managing diabetes with diet involves understanding how different foods affect your blood sugar, choosing the right types of carbohydrates, incorporating protein and healthy fats, ensuring adequate fiber intake, and timing your meals and snacks effectively. By making informed dietary choices and establishing a consistent eating routine, you can take significant steps towards controlling your blood sugar levels and improving your overall health.

Remember, small changes can make a big difference. Start by incorporating some of these strategies into your daily routine and gradually build upon them. With dedication and support, you can manage your diabetes and lead a healthy, fulfilling life. Let's embark on this journey together, one step at a time.

Chapter 3: Lifestyle Changes for Better Health

Living with type 2 diabetes requires a holistic approach that includes not just dietary changes but also adjustments in various aspects of your lifestyle. Embracing these changes can significantly improve your overall health and help you manage your diabetes more effectively. This chapter will explore the role of exercise, stress management techniques, the importance of sleep, monitoring blood sugar levels, and understanding medication and insulin. Let's dive in with a supportive and encouraging tone to help you make these practical and actionable changes.

The Role of Exercise

Exercise is a powerful tool in managing diabetes. Regular physical activity helps your body use insulin more efficiently, which can lower your blood sugar levels. It also has numerous other health benefits, such as improving cardiovascular health, aiding weight loss, and boosting mental well-being.

Types of Exercise:

1. **Aerobic Exercise:** Activities such as walking, swimming, cycling, and dancing that increase your heart rate and breathing. Aim for at least 150 minutes of moderate aerobic exercise per week, or about 30 minutes most days of the week.

2. **Strength Training:** Exercises such as lifting weights, using resistance bands, or body-weight exercises like push-ups and squats. Strength training helps build muscle, which can improve your body's ability to use glucose. Aim for strength training exercises at least twice a week.

3. **Flexibility and Balance Exercises:** Activities such as yoga, Pilates, and stretching. These exercises improve flexibility, reduce the risk of injury, and enhance overall mobility and balance.

Getting Started:

- **Set Realistic Goals:** Start with small, achievable goals and gradually increase the intensity and duration of your workouts.

- **Find Activities You Enjoy:** Exercise should be enjoyable, not a chore. Find activities that you look forward to doing.

- **Stay Consistent:** Make exercise a regular part of your routine. Consistency is key to reaping the benefits of physical activity.

- **Monitor Your Blood Sugar:** Keep an eye on your blood sugar levels before, during, and after exercise to understand how different activities affect you.

Regular exercise is a cornerstone of diabetes management. By incorporating various forms of physical activity into your routine, you can improve your health, enhance your mood, and better manage your blood sugar levels.

Stress Management Techniques

Stress can significantly impact blood sugar levels. When you're stressed, your body releases hormones such as cortisol and adrenaline, which can increase blood sugar levels. Learning to manage stress effectively is crucial for maintaining stable blood sugar levels and overall well-being.

Effective Stress Management Techniques:

1. **Mindfulness and Meditation:** Practicing mindfulness and meditation can help reduce stress and improve your emotional well-being. Even a few minutes of deep breathing or mindful meditation each day can make a big difference.

2. **Physical Activity:** Exercise is a great way to relieve stress. It releases endorphins, the body's natural stress relievers, and improves mood.

3. **Hobbies and Interests:** Engaging in activities you enjoy can provide a break from daily stressors and improve your mental health.

4. **Social Support:** Connecting with friends, family, or support groups can provide emotional support and help you cope with stress.

5. **Professional Help:** If stress becomes overwhelming, consider seeking help from a mental health professional. Therapy and counseling can provide strategies for managing stress effectively.

Practical Tips:

- **Identify Stressors:** Keep a stress diary to identify what triggers your stress and how you respond to it.

- **Develop a Routine:** Establish a daily routine that includes time for relaxation and self-care.

- **Practice Relaxation Techniques:** Techniques such as deep breathing, progressive muscle relaxation, and visualization can help calm your mind and body.

- **Get Active:** Regular physical activity can reduce stress and improve your mood.

Managing stress is an essential component of diabetes care. By incorporating stress management techniques into your daily routine, you can improve your mental and physical health and maintain better control over your blood sugar levels.

Importance of Sleep

Quality sleep is vital for everyone, but it's especially important for people with diabetes. Poor sleep can affect your body's ability to use insulin, leading to higher blood sugar levels. Additionally, lack of sleep can increase hunger and cravings for high-carbohydrate foods, further complicating diabetes management.

Benefits of Quality Sleep:

- **Improves Insulin Sensitivity:** Adequate sleep helps your body use insulin more effectively.

- **Reduces Stress:** Good sleep can lower stress levels and improve your overall mood.

- **Supports Weight Management:** Proper sleep helps regulate the hormones that control hunger and appetite.

- **Enhances Mental Clarity:** Quality sleep improves cognitive function, memory, and concentration.

Tips for Better Sleep:

1. **Establish a Sleep Routine:** Go to bed and wake up at the same time every day, even on weekends.

2. **Create a Relaxing Bedtime Ritual:** Engage in calming activities before bed, such as reading, listening to soft music, or taking a warm bath.

3. **Make Your Bedroom Sleep-Friendly:** Ensure your sleeping environment is quiet, dark, and cool. Invest in a comfortable mattress and pillows.

4. **Limit Caffeine and Alcohol:** Avoid caffeine and alcohol, especially in the hours leading up to bedtime.

5. **Reduce Screen Time:** Limit exposure to screens (TV, phone, computer) before bed, as the blue light can interfere with your sleep cycle.

Prioritizing sleep is an important part of managing diabetes. By adopting healthy sleep habits, you can improve your overall health and better control your blood sugar levels.

Monitoring Blood Sugar Levels
Regular monitoring of your blood sugar levels is crucial for effective diabetes management. It helps you understand how different foods, activities, and stress levels affect your blood sugar, allowing you to make informed decisions about your health.

Why Monitoring is Important:

- **Prevents Complications:** Regular monitoring helps you maintain blood sugar levels within your target range, reducing the risk of complications.

- **Identifies Trends:** Tracking your blood sugar levels over time can help identify patterns and trends, which can be useful for adjusting your treatment plan.

- **Informs Treatment Decisions:** Monitoring provides valuable information for you and your healthcare provider to make informed decisions about medication, diet, and exercise.

How to Monitor Blood Sugar:

1. **Self-Monitoring of Blood Glucose (SMBG):** Use a blood glucose meter to check your blood sugar levels at home. Your healthcare provider will advise how often to check your levels.

2. **Continuous Glucose Monitoring (CGM):** A CGM device tracks your blood sugar levels throughout the day and night, providing real-time data and trends.

3. **A1C Test:** This blood test, conducted by your healthcare provider, measures your average blood sugar levels over the past 2-3 months.

Practical Tips:

- **Keep a Log:** Record your blood sugar levels, along with notes about food intake, physical activity, and any stressors. This can help you and your healthcare provider make adjustments to your management plan.

- **Know Your Targets:** Work with your healthcare provider to determine your target blood sugar range and strive to stay within it.

- **Be Prepared:** Always carry your glucose meter or CGM device with you, along with a source of fast-acting glucose in case of low blood sugar.

Regular monitoring is a key aspect of diabetes management. It empowers you to take control of your health and make adjustments as needed to maintain stable blood sugar levels.

Medication and Insulin

For many people with diabetes, lifestyle changes alone may not be enough to manage blood sugar levels effectively. Medications and insulin therapy can play a crucial role in maintaining control.

Types of Medications:

1. **Oral Medications:** These include drugs that help your body use insulin more effectively, stimulate the pancreas to produce more insulin, or reduce glucose production in the liver.

2. **Injectable Medications:** In addition to insulin, there are other injectable medications that help manage blood sugar levels by mimicking the effects of certain hormones.

Insulin Therapy:

Insulin is essential for people with type 1 diabetes and may be necessary for people with type 2 diabetes if other treatments are insufficient. Insulin helps regulate blood sugar levels by allowing glucose to enter the cells.

Types of Insulin:

- **Rapid-Acting:** Starts working within minutes and lasts for a few hours. Used before meals.

- **Short-Acting:** Takes effect within 30 minutes and lasts for about 5-8 hours. Also used before meals.

- **Intermediate-Acting:** Begins working within a few hours and lasts up to 24 hours.

- **Long-Acting:** Provides a steady level of insulin throughout the day and night.

Practical Tips:

- **Follow Your Prescription:** Take medications and insulin exactly as prescribed by your healthcare provider.

- **Monitor Side Effects:** Report any side effects or concerns to your healthcare provider promptly.

- **Stay Informed:** Understand how your medications work and how to use them correctly.

- **Regular Check-Ins:** Maintain regular appointments with your healthcare provider to review your treatment plan and make adjustments as needed.

Medications and insulin are essential tools in managing diabetes. By working closely with your healthcare provider and adhering to your treatment plan, you can achieve better blood sugar control and reduce the risk of complications.

Conclusion

Making lifestyle changes to manage diabetes involves more than just diet. Incorporating regular exercise, managing stress, prioritizing sleep, monitoring blood sugar levels, and understanding the role of medications and insulin are all crucial components. These changes, though challenging, can lead to significant improvements in your health and well-being.

Remember, you are not alone in this journey. With determination, support, and the right information, you can successfully manage your diabetes and lead a healthy, fulfilling life. Let's take these steps together towards better health and well-being.

Chapter 4: Debunking Myths about Diabetes

Living with diabetes comes with a lot of misconceptions and myths that can make managing the condition more challenging. Understanding the truths about diabetes can empower you to make informed decisions about your health. Let's address some of the most common myths, uncover the truths about sugar and diabetes, explore the role of genetics, understand the connection between weight and diabetes, and debunk myths about diabetes management.

Common Misconceptions
Myth 1: Eating Too Much Sugar Causes Diabetes

One of the most pervasive myths is that eating too much sugar directly causes diabetes. While consuming high amounts of sugary foods can lead to weight gain, which is a risk factor for type 2 diabetes, sugar itself is not the direct cause.

Truth: Diabetes is caused by a combination of genetic, environmental, and lifestyle factors. For type 1 diabetes, it's an autoimmune condition where the immune system attacks insulin-producing cells. For type 2 diabetes, factors such as genetics, obesity, physical inactivity, and poor diet contribute to its development.

Myth 2: People with Diabetes Can't Eat Carbs

Another common misconception is that people with diabetes must completely avoid carbohydrates. Carbohydrates are the body's primary energy source and are essential for a balanced diet.

Truth: The key is to choose the right types of carbohydrates and monitor portion sizes. Whole grains, fruits, vegetables, and legumes are good carbohydrate sources that provide essential nutrients and fiber. Managing carb intake helps maintain stable blood sugar levels.

Myth 3: Only Overweight People Get Diabetes

While being overweight increases the risk of developing type 2 diabetes, it is not the sole cause. Many factors contribute to diabetes, and not all people with diabetes are overweight.

Truth: Genetics, age, ethnicity, and other health conditions also play significant roles in the development of diabetes. Thin or normal-weight individuals can develop diabetes, especially if they have other risk factors.

Myth 4: Diabetes is Contagious

Some people mistakenly believe that diabetes is contagious and can be spread from person to person.

Truth: Diabetes is not contagious. It cannot be transmitted through physical contact, air, or bodily fluids. It is a result of genetic and lifestyle factors.

Myth 5: People with Diabetes Can't Eat Sweets

The belief that people with diabetes must give up all sweets and desserts is another common myth.

Truth: People with diabetes can enjoy sweets in moderation. The key is to include them as part of a balanced meal plan and monitor blood sugar levels. Portion control and choosing healthier dessert options can help manage cravings without causing blood sugar spikes.

Truths About Sugar and Diabetes

The relationship between sugar and diabetes is often misunderstood. Let's clarify some important points:

Natural vs. Added Sugars:

- **Natural Sugars:** Found naturally in fruits (fructose) and dairy products (lactose). These sugars come with essential nutrients and fiber that can help moderate blood sugar levels.

- **Added Sugars:** Sugars added during processing or preparation of foods and drinks. Common sources include sugary beverages, candies, baked goods, and processed snacks. These sugars can lead to weight gain and increased risk of type 2 diabetes.

Impact on Blood Sugar Levels:

- **High Glycemic Index (GI) Foods:** Foods with high GI cause rapid spikes in blood sugar levels. Examples include sugary drinks, white bread, and pastries.

- **Low Glycemic Index (GI) Foods:** Foods with low GI are digested more slowly, causing gradual increases in blood sugar levels. Examples include whole grains, fruits, and legumes.

Moderation is Key:

While it's important to limit added sugars, it's not necessary to eliminate them entirely. The focus should be on a balanced diet that includes a variety of nutrient-dense foods.

Label Reading:

Reading nutrition labels can help you identify added sugars in packaged foods. Look for terms such as sucrose, high-fructose corn syrup, and dextrose. Aim to choose products with minimal added sugars.

The Role of Genetics

Genetics play a crucial role in the development of diabetes, particularly type 1 diabetes and type 2 diabetes.

Type 1 Diabetes:

- **Genetic Predisposition:** A family history of type 1 diabetes increases the risk. Certain genes have been identified that are associated with a higher risk of developing type 1 diabetes.

- **Environmental Triggers:** In addition to genetics, environmental factors such as viral infections may trigger the autoimmune response that leads to type 1 diabetes.

Type 2 Diabetes:

- **Family History:** Having a parent or sibling with type 2 diabetes significantly increases the risk. However, genetics alone do not determine whether someone will develop type 2 diabetes.

- **Lifestyle Factors:** Obesity, poor diet, and physical inactivity can interact with genetic predispositions to increase the risk of developing type 2 diabetes.

Genetic Testing:

Genetic testing can provide information about the risk of developing diabetes, but it is not commonly used in routine clinical practice. Understanding your family history and discussing it with your healthcare provider can help assess your risk and guide preventive measures.

Weight and Diabetes

Weight plays a significant role in the development and management of type 2 diabetes. However, it's important to understand the nuances of this relationship.

Impact of Obesity:

- **Insulin Resistance:** Excess body fat, particularly around the abdomen, can cause cells to become resistant to insulin, leading to higher blood sugar levels.

- **Inflammation:** Obesity is associated with chronic low-grade inflammation, which can interfere with insulin action.

Weight Loss Benefits:

- **Improved Insulin Sensitivity:** Losing even a small amount of weight can improve insulin sensitivity and help lower blood sugar levels.

- **Reduced Medication Need:** Weight loss can reduce the need for diabetes medications and improve overall health outcomes.

Healthy Weight Management:

- **Balanced Diet:** Focus on a balanced diet rich in whole foods, vegetables, fruits, lean proteins, and healthy fats.

- **Regular Exercise:** Incorporate regular physical activity to aid weight loss and improve insulin sensitivity.

- **Behavioral Changes:** Adopt sustainable lifestyle changes rather than quick-fix diets. Small, consistent changes can lead to long-term success.

Support and Resources:

Seek support from healthcare providers, dietitians, and support groups. Having a support system can provide motivation and accountability.

Myths About Diabetes Management
Myth 1: Insulin is a Sign of Failure

Some people believe that needing insulin means they have failed in managing their diabetes.

Truth: Diabetes is a progressive disease, and the need for insulin can be part of its natural progression. Insulin is a vital tool for managing blood sugar levels and preventing complications. It's not a sign of failure but a necessary part of treatment for many people.

Myth 2: You Can Cure Diabetes with Diet and Exercise Alone

While diet and exercise are critical components of diabetes management, they are not cures.

Truth: Type 1 diabetes cannot be cured, and while lifestyle changes can significantly improve type 2 diabetes management, they do not cure the disease. Medications, including insulin, may still be necessary for effective management.

Myth 3: People with Diabetes Should Eat Special Diabetic Foods

There is a misconception that people with diabetes need to eat special foods labeled as "diabetic" or "sugar-free."

Truth: A healthy diet for people with diabetes is similar to that recommended for the general population. Focus on whole, unprocessed foods, and avoid products that may be marketed as diabetic-friendly but contain unhealthy substitutes or additives.

Myth 4: You Can't Live a Normal Life with Diabetes

Some believe that diabetes severely limits life activities and enjoyment.

Truth: With proper management, people with diabetes can lead full, active lives. Education, self-care, and support are key to successful diabetes management. Advances in diabetes care, including new medications and technologies, have made it easier than ever to manage the condition effectively.

Conclusion

Understanding and debunking myths about diabetes is essential for effective management and improving your quality of life. By dispelling these misconceptions, you can focus on the facts and make informed decisions about your health. Remember, you are not alone on this journey. With the right information, support, and strategies, you can manage your diabetes and lead a healthy, fulfilling life. Let's move forward with confidence and clarity, embracing the truths about diabetes and leaving the myths behind.

Chapter 5: Smart Grocery Shopping for Diabetes

Navigating the grocery store and planning your meals can be an empowering step toward managing your diabetes. With a little preparation and knowledge, you can make choices that support your health and keep your blood sugar levels stable. This chapter will guide you through planning your shopping list, navigating the grocery store, making healthy substitutions, buying in bulk and storing food properly, and incorporating seasonal and local produce into your diet.

Planning Your Shopping List
Creating a detailed shopping list is the first step to successful grocery shopping. A well-thought-out list helps you stay focused, saves time, and ensures you buy only what you need, reducing the temptation to purchase unhealthy options.

Steps to Plan Your Shopping List:

1. **Plan Your Meals:** Start by planning your meals for the week. Include breakfast, lunch, dinner, and snacks. Consider balanced meals that incorporate whole grains, lean proteins, healthy fats, and plenty of vegetables.

2. **Check Your Pantry:** Before you head to the store, check what you already have. This prevents you from buying duplicates and helps you use up items you already have.

3. **Categorize Your List:** Organize your list by sections of the grocery store—produce, dairy, meat, pantry items, etc. This makes shopping quicker and more efficient.

4. **Include Healthy Staples:** Ensure your list includes diabetes-friendly staples such as whole grains, fresh vegetables, lean meats, legumes, and low-fat dairy products.

5. **Stick to the List:** Avoid impulse purchases by sticking to your list. If you see something that's not on your list but want to try, think about how it fits into your meal plan before adding it to your cart.

Example Shopping List:

- **Produce:** Spinach, kale, bell peppers, tomatoes, carrots, apples, berries, avocados

- **Grains:** Quinoa, brown rice, whole grain bread, oats

- **Proteins:** Chicken breast, lean ground turkey, eggs, tofu, lentils

- **Dairy:** Greek yogurt, low-fat milk, cheese

- **Pantry:** Olive oil, nuts, seeds, canned beans, spices

- **Frozen:** Frozen vegetables, fish fillets

Navigating the Grocery Store

Understanding how to navigate the grocery store can help you make healthier choices and avoid processed foods that can spike your blood sugar levels.

Tips for Navigating the Grocery Store:

1. **Shop the Perimeter:** Most grocery stores are designed with fresh produce, dairy, meat, and seafood around the perimeter. These sections usually contain less processed and healthier options.

2. **Read Labels:** When you venture into the aisles, make it a habit to read nutrition labels. Look for items low in added sugars, saturated fats, and sodium. Pay attention to serving sizes and the ingredient list.

3. **Avoid the Temptation Aisles:** Steer clear of aisles that contain snacks, sweets, and sugary beverages. These are often high in empty calories and can destabilize your blood sugar levels.

4. **Choose Whole Foods:** Opt for whole, unprocessed foods whenever possible. Fresh fruits and vegetables, lean meats, whole grains, and low-fat dairy are better choices than processed foods.

5. **Stay Informed:** Know which foods to avoid and which ones are beneficial for managing diabetes. Foods high in fiber, low in saturated fats, and with low glycemic indices are generally good choices.

Healthy Substitutions

Making healthy substitutions in your diet can significantly impact your blood sugar management and overall health. Here are some practical swaps you can make:

Substitutions for Carbohydrates:

- **White Rice:** Replace with brown rice, quinoa, or cauliflower rice.

- **White Bread:** Opt for whole grain or sprouted grain bread.

- **Pasta:** Choose whole grain pasta, zucchini noodles, or spaghetti squash.

Substitutions for Fats:

- **Butter:** Use olive oil or avocado oil for cooking.

- **Cream:** Replace with Greek yogurt or a plant-based milk like almond or coconut milk.

Substitutions for Sweets:

- **Sugar:** Use natural sweeteners like stevia, monk fruit, or small amounts of honey.

- **Soda:** Replace with sparkling water infused with fresh fruit.

Substitutions for Snacks:

- **Chips:** Swap for air-popped popcorn, raw veggies with hummus, or nuts.

- **Candy:** Replace with fresh or dried fruits (in moderation).

These small changes can make a big difference in managing your diabetes without sacrificing flavor or enjoyment.

Buying in Bulk and Storage Tips

Buying in bulk can save money and ensure you always have healthy options on hand. However, it's essential to know how to store these items properly to maintain their nutritional value and prevent spoilage.

Benefits of Buying in Bulk:

- **Cost Savings:** Bulk items are often cheaper per unit than smaller packages.
- **Convenience:** Having staples on hand reduces the need for frequent shopping trips.
- **Reduced Packaging Waste:** Buying in bulk can reduce the amount of packaging waste.

Smart Bulk Buying Tips:

1. **Choose Non-Perishables:** Items like grains, beans, nuts, seeds, and canned goods are excellent choices for bulk buying.
2. **Freeze Perishables:** Meat, bread, and some fruits and vegetables can be frozen to extend their shelf life.
3. **Store Properly:** Use airtight containers to store bulk items and keep them fresh. Label containers with dates to ensure you use older items first.

Storage Tips:

- **Grains and Legumes:** Store in airtight containers in a cool, dark place.
- **Nuts and Seeds:** Keep in the refrigerator or freezer to prevent them from going rancid.
- **Meat and Fish:** Divide into portions and freeze in airtight bags or containers.
- **Fruits and Vegetables:** Store appropriately (e.g., some in the fridge, some on the counter) and use produce bins to keep them fresh longer.

Incorporating Seasonal and Local Produce

Eating seasonal and local produce not only supports local farmers but also ensures that you are consuming the freshest, most nutrient-dense foods available.

Benefits of Seasonal and Local Produce:

- **Better Flavor and Nutrition:** Fruits and vegetables are often fresher and more flavorful when eaten in season.
- **Environmental Impact:** Local produce requires less transportation, reducing carbon footprint.
- **Cost-Effective:** Seasonal produce is often less expensive due to abundance and lower transportation costs.

Tips for Incorporating Seasonal Produce:

1. **Visit Farmers' Markets:** Local markets are a great place to find fresh, seasonal produce. Engage with farmers to learn more about how the produce is grown.

2. **Join a CSA:** Community Supported Agriculture (CSA) programs allow you to subscribe to a farm and receive regular boxes of seasonal produce.

3. **Grow Your Own:** If you have space, consider starting a small garden. Growing your own vegetables can be rewarding and ensures you have fresh produce at your fingertips.

4. **Seasonal Guides:** Use seasonal produce guides to plan your shopping and meals around what's fresh and in season.

Examples of Seasonal Produce:

- **Spring:** Asparagus, peas, strawberries, radishes

- **Summer:** Tomatoes, zucchini, berries, bell peppers

- **Fall:** Pumpkins, squash, apples, Brussels sprouts

- **Winter:** Kale, citrus fruits, sweet potatoes, turnips

Incorporating seasonal and local produce into your diet can enhance your meals with fresh flavors and high nutritional value, making healthy eating more enjoyable and sustainable.

Conclusion

Smart grocery shopping is a cornerstone of managing diabetes effectively. By planning your shopping list, navigating the store wisely, making healthy substitutions, buying in bulk, and incorporating seasonal produce, you can create a diet that supports your health and keeps your blood sugar levels stable. Remember, every small step you take towards healthier eating habits makes a significant difference in managing your diabetes and improving your overall well-being. Happy shopping!

From Learning to Cooking

You've made it through the first section of this book, where we delved deeply into understanding type 2 diabetes. We've explored the basics of the disease, how diet and lifestyle changes can play a pivotal role in managing it, and debunked common myths that often surround diabetes. You've learned about the importance of monitoring blood sugar levels, the role of medication, and the impact of stress, sleep, and exercise on your health. Now, it's time to take that foundational knowledge and put it into action in the kitchen.

Bridging Knowledge with Practice

The first section provided you with a strong foundation of knowledge about diabetes. Understanding the "why" behind dietary choices is crucial for making informed decisions. But knowledge alone isn't enough. It's the practical application of this knowledge that leads to meaningful change. This is where the second section of the book comes into play.

Cooking and eating healthfully shouldn't be a chore; it should be an enjoyable part of your life. The recipes in this book are designed not only to be diabetes-friendly but also delicious and satisfying. Whether you're a seasoned cook or a beginner, you'll find recipes that suit your taste and skill level.

Translating Nutritional Knowledge into Daily Meals

In Section 1, we discussed the importance of various nutrients and how they affect blood sugar levels. Now, we will translate that understanding into everyday meals that you can prepare at home. Here's a quick recap of what you've learned and how it will be applied in the recipes:

Carbohydrates and Glycemic Index:

- You've learned that not all carbs are created equal. Low glycemic index (GI) foods are digested more slowly and cause a gradual rise in blood sugar levels, making them better choices for people with diabetes.

- The recipes will include a variety of low GI foods, helping you maintain stable blood sugar levels throughout the day.

Protein and Fat Considerations:

- Protein is crucial for maintaining muscle mass and providing satiety. Healthy fats are important for heart health and also help in managing blood sugar levels.

- Each recipe balances protein and healthy fats with carbohydrates to create well-rounded meals that are both nutritious and satisfying.

The Importance of Fiber:

- Fiber plays a key role in digestion and blood sugar control. High-fiber foods help slow down the absorption of sugar, preventing spikes in blood sugar levels.

- Many recipes incorporate high-fiber ingredients such as vegetables, whole grains, and legumes to help you meet your daily fiber needs.

Practical Tips for the Kitchen

Before diving into the recipes, let's discuss some practical tips that will help you make the most of your time in the kitchen:

Meal Planning and Prep:

- Planning your meals in advance can save time and ensure you have all the ingredients you need. Consider setting aside some time each week to plan your meals and create a shopping list.

- Meal prep can be a game-changer. Preparing ingredients or whole meals in advance can make healthy eating more convenient, especially on busy days.

Reading Recipes and Labels:

- When trying new recipes, read through the entire recipe before you start cooking. This helps you understand the steps and ensures you have all the necessary ingredients and tools.

- Reading food labels is essential, especially when it comes to packaged foods. Look for hidden sugars, unhealthy fats, and high sodium content.

Cooking Techniques:

- Use healthy cooking techniques such as grilling, baking, steaming, and sautéing with minimal oil. These methods help retain nutrients and reduce the need for added fats.

- Experiment with herbs and spices to add flavor without adding extra calories or sodium. Fresh herbs, garlic, ginger, and spices like turmeric and cumin can enhance the taste of your dishes while providing additional health benefits.

Making Mealtime Enjoyable

Healthy eating should be enjoyable and not feel restrictive. Here are a few ways to make mealtime more enjoyable:

Variety and Balance:

- Variety is the spice of life. Don't be afraid to try new ingredients and recipes. Mixing things up can keep meals exciting and prevent boredom.

- Balance your meals by including a variety of food groups. Aim for a colorful plate with plenty of vegetables, lean proteins, whole grains, and healthy fats.

Mindful Eating:

- Practice mindful eating by paying attention to your hunger and fullness cues. Eat slowly and savor each bite. This can help prevent overeating and make meals more satisfying.

- Avoid distractions like TV or smartphones during meals. Focus on your food and the experience of eating.

Family and Social Meals:

- Involve your family in meal planning and preparation. This can be a great way to educate them about healthy eating and ensure everyone is on board with the changes.

- Don't let diabetes prevent you from enjoying social meals. Communicate your needs to friends and family, and don't hesitate to bring a diabetes-friendly dish to gatherings.

Looking Ahead to Delicious Diabetes-Friendly Recipes

Now that you have a solid understanding of diabetes management and practical tips for the kitchen, you're ready to explore the delicious recipes in the second section of this book. These recipes are designed to be simple, nutritious, and enjoyable. They will help you put into practice the dietary principles you've learned and make healthy eating a regular part of your life.

Each recipe includes detailed instructions, nutritional information, and tips to make the cooking process smooth and enjoyable. Whether you're looking for a quick breakfast, a satisfying lunch, a hearty dinner, or a delicious dessert, you'll find a variety of options to suit your needs.

Remember, managing diabetes is a journey, and every small step you take towards healthier eating is a step in the right direction. Use this book as your guide and companion on this journey. With the right tools and knowledge, you can make positive changes that support your health and well-being.

Let's embark on this culinary adventure together, starting with the first recipe. Happy cooking!

Section Two: Delicious Diabetes-Friendly Recipes

Chapter 6: Breakfast Bonanza

Breakfast is often heralded as the most important meal of the day, and for good reason. Starting your day with a nutritious meal can set the tone for sustained energy, improved mood, and better overall health. For those managing type 2 diabetes, a healthy breakfast is even more critical, as it helps maintain stable blood sugar levels and prevents mid-morning energy crashes. This chapter is packed with a variety of delicious, diabetes-friendly breakfast recipes that are both satisfying and easy to prepare.

1. Greek Yogurt Parfait with Berries

Greek yogurt is an excellent choice for breakfast due to its high protein content and low glycemic index. This parfait pairs creamy yogurt with the natural sweetness of berries and the crunch of nuts and seeds.

Servings: 1
Preparation Time: 5 minutes
Cooking Time: None
Ingredients:

- 1 cup (240 ml) plain Greek yogurt
- 1/2 cup (75 g) mixed berries (strawberries, blueberries, raspberries)
- 1 tablespoon (15 ml) chia seeds or flaxseeds
- 1 tablespoon (15 ml) sliced almonds or walnuts
- Optional: Drizzle of honey or agave nectar

Instructions:

1. Layer Greek yogurt, berries, chia seeds, and almonds in a bowl or parfait glass.
2. Repeat layers as desired.
3. Serve immediately or refrigerate.

2. Veggie Omelette

Packed with protein and vegetables, this veggie omelette is a great way to start your day with a boost of nutrients and energy.

Servings: 1
Preparation Time: 10 minutes
Cooking Time: 10 minutes

Ingredients:

- 2 large eggs
- 1/4 cup (35 g) diced bell peppers
- 1/4 cup (30 g) chopped spinach
- 1/4 cup (30 g) diced tomatoes
- 1/4 cup (30 g) diced onions
- Salt and pepper to taste
- 1 tablespoon (15 ml) olive oil

Instructions:

1. Whisk eggs with salt and pepper.
2. Sauté onions and bell peppers in olive oil until soft.
3. Add spinach and tomatoes until spinach wilts.
4. Pour eggs over vegetables and cook until set.
5. Fold omelette and serve.

3. Chia Seed Pudding

Chia seeds are a powerhouse of fiber and omega-3 fatty acids, making them an excellent choice for a diabetes-friendly breakfast.

Servings: 2
Preparation Time: 5 minutes
Cooking Time: None (Refrigeration: 2 hours)
Ingredients:

- 1/4 cup (40 g) chia seeds
- 1 cup (240 ml) unsweetened almond milk
- 1 teaspoon (5 ml) vanilla extract
- 1 tablespoon (15 ml) maple syrup or sweetener of choice

- Fresh fruit for topping (optional)

Instructions:
1. Mix chia seeds, almond milk, vanilla extract, and sweetener.
2. Let sit for 5 minutes, stir, and refrigerate for at least 2 hours or overnight.
3. Stir and top with fruit before serving.

4. Whole Grain Avocado Toast

Whole grain bread and avocado make a nutritious and satisfying breakfast, rich in fiber and healthy fats.

Servings: 2
Preparation Time: 5 minutes
Cooking Time: 5 minutes
Ingredients:
- 2 slices whole grain bread
- 1 ripe avocado
- Salt and pepper to taste
- Optional: Sliced cherry tomatoes, red pepper flakes, or poached egg

Instructions:
1. Toast bread.
2. Mash avocado with salt and pepper.
3. Spread avocado on toast and top with optional ingredients.
4. Serve immediately.

5. Smoothie Bowls

Smoothie bowls are a fun and versatile breakfast option that can be tailored to your taste and nutritional needs.

Servings: 1
Preparation Time: 5 minutes
Cooking Time: None
Ingredients:
- 1 frozen banana
- 1/2 cup (75 g) frozen berries
- 1/2 cup (120 ml) unsweetened almond milk
- 1 tablespoon (15 ml) almond butter
- Toppings: Fresh fruit, granola, chia seeds, nuts

Instructions:
1. Blend banana, berries, almond milk, and almond butter until smooth.
2. Pour into a bowl and add toppings.
3. Serve immediately.

6. Cottage Cheese with Fresh Fruit

Cottage cheese is a high-protein, low-carb option that pairs well with a variety of fruits for a quick and healthy breakfast.

Servings: 1
Preparation Time: 5 minutes
Cooking Time: None
Ingredients:
- 1 cup (240 g) cottage cheese
- 1/2 cup (75 g) fresh fruit (pineapple, berries, melon)
- 1 tablespoon (15 ml) honey or agave nectar (optional)
- 1 tablespoon (15 ml) chopped nuts (optional)

Instructions:
1. Scoop cottage cheese into a bowl.
2. Top with fresh fruit, honey, and nuts.
3. Serve immediately.

7. Almond Flour Pancakes

These gluten-free pancakes are a delicious and diabetes-friendly alternative to traditional pancakes.

Servings: 4
Preparation Time: 10 minutes
Cooking Time: 15 minutes
Ingredients:
- 1 cup (120 g) almond flour
- 1/4 cup (60 ml) unsweetened almond milk
- 2 large eggs
- 1 tablespoon (15 ml) maple syrup or sweetener of choice
- 1 teaspoon (5 ml) vanilla extract
- 1/2 teaspoon (2.5 g) baking powder
- A pinch of salt

- Cooking spray or oil for the pan

Instructions:
1. Whisk together almond flour, baking powder, and salt.
2. Mix eggs, almond milk, maple syrup, and vanilla.
3. Combine wet and dry ingredients.
4. Cook pancakes in a heated skillet until bubbles form, then flip.
5. Serve with fruit and syrup.

8. Quinoa Breakfast Bowl

Quinoa is a high-protein grain that makes for a hearty and nutritious breakfast bowl.

Servings: 1
Preparation Time: 5 minutes
Cooking Time: None (assuming quinoa is pre-cooked)
Ingredients:
- 1/2 cup (90 g) cooked quinoa
- 1/4 cup (37.5 g) fresh berries
- 1/2 banana, sliced
- 1 tablespoon (15 ml) almond butter
- 1 teaspoon (5 ml) honey or maple syrup
- A sprinkle of chia seeds

Instructions:
1. Place quinoa in a bowl.
2. Top with berries, banana, almond butter, and chia seeds.
3. Drizzle with honey or syrup.
4. Serve immediately.

9. Scrambled Tofu

Scrambled tofu is a great plant-based alternative to scrambled eggs, high in protein and versatile in flavor.

Servings: 2
Preparation Time: 10 minutes
Cooking Time: 10 minutes
Ingredients:
- 1 block (400 g) firm tofu, drained and crumbled
- 1/4 cup (30 g) diced onions
- 1/4 cup (35 g) diced bell peppers
- 1/4 cup (30 g) chopped spinach
- 1 tablespoon (15 ml) olive oil
- 1/2 teaspoon (2.5 g) turmeric
- 1/2 teaspoon (2.5 g) garlic powder
- Salt and pepper to taste

Instructions:
1. Heat olive oil and sauté onions and bell peppers.
2. Add crumbled tofu, turmeric, garlic powder, salt, and pepper.
3. Cook for 5-7 minutes, then add spinach until wilted.
4. Serve hot.

10. Overnight Oats

Overnight oats are an easy, make-ahead breakfast option that's both nutritious and customizable.

Servings: 1
Preparation Time: 5 minutes
Cooking Time: None (Refrigeration: overnight)
Ingredients:
- 1/2 cup (45 g) rolled oats
- 1/2 cup (120 ml) unsweetened almond milk
- 1/4 cup (60 g) Greek yogurt
- 1 tablespoon (15 ml) chia seeds
- 1 teaspoon (5 ml) honey or maple syrup
- Toppings: Fresh fruit, nuts, seeds

Instructions:
1. Combine oats, almond milk, yogurt, chia seeds, and honey.
2. Stir, cover, and refrigerate overnight.
3. Add toppings in the morning and enjoy.

11. Breakfast Burritos

A savory and portable breakfast option, these burritos are packed with protein and veggies.

Servings: 2
Preparation Time: 10 minutes
Cooking Time: 10 minutes
Ingredients:
- 2 large eggs

- 1/4 cup (30 g) diced bell peppers
- 1/4 cup (30 g) diced onions
- 1/4 cup (30 g) chopped spinach
- 1/4 cup (60 g) black beans, drained and rinsed
- 2 whole grain tortillas
- 1 tablespoon (15 ml) olive oil
- Salt and pepper to taste
- Salsa and avocado for serving (optional)

Instructions:

1. Heat olive oil in a skillet over medium heat.
2. Sauté onions and bell peppers until soft.
3. Add spinach and black beans, cooking until the spinach wilts.
4. In a bowl, whisk the eggs with salt and pepper, then pour into the skillet.
5. Cook until the eggs are scrambled and fully cooked.
6. Divide the mixture between the tortillas, wrap them up, and serve with salsa and avocado if desired.

12. Berry Breakfast Muffins

These muffins are perfect for a quick and healthy breakfast on the go.

Servings: 12
Preparation Time: 15 minutes
Cooking Time: 20-25 minutes
Ingredients:

- 1 1/2 cups (180 g) whole wheat flour
- 1/2 cup (120 ml) unsweetened applesauce
- 1/2 cup (100 g) fresh or frozen berries
- 1/2 cup (120 ml) unsweetened almond milk
- 1/4 cup (60 ml) honey or maple syrup
- 1 large egg
- 1 teaspoon (5 ml) vanilla extract
- 1 teaspoon (5 g) baking powder
- 1/2 teaspoon (2.5 g) baking soda
- A pinch of salt

Instructions:

1. Preheat the oven to 350°F (175°C) and line a muffin tin with paper liners.
2. In a large bowl, mix the flour, baking powder, baking soda, and salt.
3. In another bowl, whisk the egg, applesauce, almond milk, honey, and vanilla extract.
4. Combine the wet and dry ingredients, then fold in the berries.
5. Divide the batter evenly among the muffin cups.
6. Bake for 20-25 minutes or until a toothpick inserted into the center comes out clean.
7. Allow to cool before serving.

13. Spinach and Feta Frittata

This frittata is a tasty way to include more greens in your breakfast.

Servings: 4
Preparation Time: 10 minutes
Cooking Time: 20 minutes
Ingredients:

- 6 large eggs
- 1 cup (30 g) fresh spinach, chopped
- 1/2 cup (75 g) crumbled feta cheese
- 1/4 cup (30 g) diced onions
- 1/4 cup (30 g) diced bell peppers
- 1 tablespoon (15 ml) olive oil
- Salt and pepper to taste

Instructions:

1. Preheat the oven to 350°F (175°C).
2. Heat olive oil in an oven-safe skillet over medium heat.
3. Sauté the onions and bell peppers until soft.
4. Add the spinach and cook until wilted.
5. In a bowl, whisk the eggs with salt and pepper.
6. Pour the eggs into the skillet and stir to combine with the vegetables.
7. Sprinkle the feta cheese on top.

8. Transfer the skillet to the oven and bake for 15-20 minutes or until the eggs are set.
9. Slice and serve.

14. Nut Butter and Banana Wrap

This quick and easy wrap is perfect for a nutritious start to the day.

Servings: 1
Preparation Time: 5 minutes
Cooking Time: None
Ingredients:

- 1 whole grain tortilla
- 2 tablespoons (30 g) almond or peanut butter
- 1 banana, sliced
- A sprinkle of chia seeds

Instructions:

1. Spread the nut butter evenly over the tortilla.
2. Place the banana slices in a line down the center.
3. Sprinkle with chia seeds.
4. Roll up the tortilla, slice in half, and serve.

15. Savory Oatmeal

A savory twist on traditional oatmeal, this dish is both hearty and healthy.

Servings: 1
Preparation Time: 5 minutes
Cooking Time: 10 minutes
Ingredients:

- 1/2 cup (45 g) rolled oats
- 1 cup (240 ml) water or unsweetened almond milk
- 1/4 cup (30 g) diced tomatoes
- 1/4 cup (30 g) chopped spinach
- 1 large egg
- 1 tablespoon (15 ml) olive oil
- Salt and pepper to taste

Instructions:

1. Cook the oats in water or almond milk according to package instructions.
2. While the oats are cooking, heat olive oil in a skillet over medium heat.
3. Sauté the tomatoes and spinach until the spinach is wilted.
4. Fry the egg in the same skillet to your desired doneness.
5. Combine the cooked oats with the sautéed vegetables.
6. Top with the fried egg, and season with salt and pepper before serving.

16. Egg Muffins

These portable egg muffins are perfect for meal prep and busy mornings.

Servings: 12
Preparation Time: 10 minutes
Cooking Time: 25 minutes
Ingredients:

- 6 large eggs
- 1/4 cup (60 ml) unsweetened almond milk
- 1/4 cup (30 g) diced bell peppers
- 1/4 cup (30 g) diced onions
- 1/4 cup (30 g) chopped spinach
- 1/4 cup (30 g) shredded cheese (optional)
- Salt and pepper to taste

Instructions:

1. Preheat the oven to 350°F (175°C) and grease a muffin tin.
2. In a bowl, whisk together the eggs, almond milk, salt, and pepper.
3. Stir in the bell peppers, onions, spinach, and cheese (if using).
4. Pour the mixture into the muffin tin, filling each cup about 3/4 full.
5. Bake for 20-25 minutes or until the eggs are set.
6. Allow to cool before removing from the tin.

17. Buckwheat Pancakes

Buckwheat flour makes these pancakes a nutritious and gluten-free breakfast option.

Servings: 4
Preparation Time: 10 minutes
Cooking Time: 15 minutes
Ingredients:

- 1 cup (120 g) buckwheat flour
- 1 cup (240 ml) unsweetened almond milk
- 1 large egg
- 1 tablespoon (15 ml) honey or maple syrup
- 1 teaspoon (5 ml) vanilla extract
- 1/2 teaspoon (2.5 g) baking powder
- A pinch of salt
- Cooking spray or oil for the pan

Instructions:

1. In a bowl, whisk together the buckwheat flour, baking powder, and salt.
2. In another bowl, mix the egg, almond milk, honey, and vanilla extract.
3. Combine the wet and dry ingredients, stirring until just combined.
4. Heat a non-stick skillet over medium heat and coat with cooking spray or oil.
5. Pour 1/4 cup (60 ml) of batter onto the skillet for each pancake. Cook until bubbles form on the surface, then flip and cook until golden brown.
6. Serve with fresh fruit and a drizzle of syrup or yogurt.

18. Breakfast Salad

A fresh and healthy start to your day, this salad is full of nutrients and flavor.

Servings: 1
Preparation Time: 10 minutes
Cooking Time: None
Ingredients:

- 2 cups (60 g) mixed greens
- 1/4 cup (30 g) cherry tomatoes, halved
- 1/4 cup (30 g) cucumber, sliced
- 1/4 cup (30 g) avocado, diced
- 2 boiled eggs, sliced
- 1 tablespoon (15 ml) olive oil
- 1 tablespoon (15 ml) balsamic vinegar
- Salt and pepper to taste

Instructions:

1. In a large bowl, combine the mixed greens, cherry tomatoes, cucumber, and avocado.
2. Top with the sliced boiled eggs.
3. Drizzle with olive oil and balsamic vinegar.
4. Season with salt and pepper.
5. Toss gently and serve immediately.

19. Spiced Apple Compote

A warm and comforting breakfast topping that pairs well with yogurt, oatmeal, or pancakes.

Servings: 4
Preparation Time: 10 minutes
Cooking Time: 15 minutes
Ingredients:

- 2 apples, peeled, cored, and diced
- 1 tablespoon (15 ml) lemon juice
- 1 tablespoon (15 ml) water
- 1 teaspoon (5 g) cinnamon
- 1/2 teaspoon (2.5 g) nutmeg
- 1 tablespoon (15 ml) maple syrup or honey

Instructions:

1. Combine apples, lemon juice, water, cinnamon, and nutmeg in a saucepan.
2. Cook over medium heat, stirring occasionally, until apples are soft and mixture is thickened, about 10-15 minutes.
3. Stir in maple syrup or honey.
4. Serve warm over yogurt, oatmeal, or pancakes.

20. Muesli Mix

A versatile and nutritious breakfast option that can be prepared in advance.

Servings: 4
Preparation Time: 10 minutes
Cooking Time: None
Ingredients:

- 2 cups (180 g) rolled oats
- 1/2 cup (75 g) dried fruit (raisins, cranberries, apricots)
- 1/2 cup (60 g) nuts and seeds (almonds, sunflower seeds, chia seeds)
- 1/4 cup (30 g) shredded coconut
- 1 teaspoon (5 g) cinnamon
- 1/2 teaspoon (2.5 g) nutmeg

Instructions:

1. Combine rolled oats, dried fruit, nuts, seeds, shredded coconut, cinnamon, and nutmeg in a large bowl.
2. Mix well to combine.
3. Store in an airtight container.
4. Serve with milk or yogurt.

Chapter 7: Light and Lively Lunches

Lunch is an important meal that can rejuvenate you for the rest of the day. For those managing diabetes, it's essential to have lunches that are balanced, nourishing, and delicious. This chapter includes a variety of light yet satisfying lunch options that help maintain stable blood sugar levels while providing essential nutrients.

21. Grilled Chicken Salad
A hearty yet light salad that combines lean protein with fresh vegetables.
Servings: 2
Preparation Time: 10 minutes
Cooking Time: 10 minutes
Ingredients:
- 1 grilled chicken breast, sliced
- 2 cups (60 g) mixed greens
- 1/2 cup (75 g) cherry tomatoes, halved
- 1/4 cup (30 g) cucumber, sliced
- 1/4 cup (30 g) red onion, thinly sliced
- 1/4 cup (30 g) feta cheese, crumbled
- 1 tablespoon (15 ml) olive oil
- 1 tablespoon (15 ml) balsamic vinegar
- Salt and pepper to taste

Instructions:
1. Arrange mixed greens on a plate.
2. Top with grilled chicken, cherry tomatoes, cucumber, red onion, and feta cheese.
3. Drizzle with olive oil and balsamic vinegar.
4. Season with salt and pepper.
5. Toss gently and serve.

22. Lentil Soup
A warming and nutritious soup rich in fiber and protein.
Servings: 4
Preparation Time: 15 minutes
Cooking Time: 30 minutes
Ingredients:
- 1 cup (200 g) dried lentils, rinsed
- 1 onion, diced
- 2 carrots, sliced
- 2 celery stalks, sliced
- 2 garlic cloves, minced
- 1 can (400 g) diced tomatoes
- 4 cups (1 liter) vegetable broth
- 1 teaspoon (5 g) cumin
- 1 teaspoon (5 g) thyme
- Salt and pepper to taste

Instructions:
1. In a large pot, sauté onion, carrots, celery, and garlic until softened.
2. Add lentils, diced tomatoes, vegetable broth, cumin, and thyme.
3. Bring to a boil, then reduce heat and simmer for 30 minutes or until lentils are tender.
4. Season with salt and pepper.
5. Serve hot.

23. Quinoa and Black Bean Bowl
A protein-packed bowl that's both filling and nutritious.
Servings: 2
Preparation Time: 10 minutes
Cooking Time: 15 minutes
Ingredients:
- 1 cup (185 g) cooked quinoa
- 1 cup (240 g) black beans, drained and rinsed
- 1/2 cup (75 g) corn kernels
- 1/2 cup (75 g) diced tomatoes
- 1/4 cup (30 g) diced red onion
- 1 avocado, diced
- 1 tablespoon (15 ml) lime juice
- 1 tablespoon (15 ml) olive oil
- Salt and pepper to taste

Instructions:

1. In a large bowl, combine quinoa, black beans, corn, tomatoes, and red onion.
2. Drizzle with lime juice and olive oil.
3. Toss gently and season with salt and pepper.
4. Top with diced avocado.
5. Serve immediately.

24. Veggie Stir-Fry

A colorful and quick stir-fry packed with fresh vegetables.

Servings: 2
Preparation Time: 10 minutes
Cooking Time: 10 minutes
Ingredients:

- 1 cup (150 g) broccoli florets
- 1 red bell pepper, sliced
- 1 yellow bell pepper, sliced
- 1 cup (150 g) snap peas
- 1 carrot, sliced
- 2 tablespoons (30 ml) soy sauce
- 1 tablespoon (15 ml) sesame oil
- 1 tablespoon (15 ml) olive oil
- 1 garlic clove, minced
- 1 teaspoon (5 g) ginger, minced
- Optional: Sesame seeds for garnish

Instructions:

1. Heat olive oil in a large skillet over medium-high heat.
2. Add garlic and ginger, sauté for 1 minute.
3. Add broccoli, bell peppers, snap peas, and carrot. Stir-fry for 5-7 minutes.
4. Add soy sauce and sesame oil, stirring to combine.
5. Cook for another 2-3 minutes until vegetables are tender.
6. Garnish with sesame seeds if desired.
7. Serve hot.

25. Turkey and Avocado Wrap

A quick and satisfying wrap that's perfect for lunch on the go.

Servings: 2
Preparation Time: 10 minutes
Cooking Time: None
Ingredients:

- 2 whole grain tortillas
- 4 slices turkey breast
- 1 avocado, sliced
- 1/2 cup (75 g) shredded lettuce
- 1/4 cup (30 g) shredded cheese
- 1/4 cup (60 g) salsa
- Salt and pepper to taste

Instructions:

1. Lay tortillas flat and layer with turkey, avocado, lettuce, cheese, and salsa.
2. Season with salt and pepper.
3. Roll up tortillas tightly.
4. Slice in half and serve.

26. Cauliflower Rice Salad

A light and refreshing salad that's low in carbs but high in flavor.

Servings: 2
Preparation Time: 15 minutes
Cooking Time: 5 minutes
Ingredients:

- 1 small head cauliflower, grated into rice-sized pieces
- 1/2 cup (75 g) cherry tomatoes, halved
- 1/2 cucumber, diced
- 1/4 cup (30 g) red onion, diced
- 1/4 cup (30 g) fresh parsley, chopped
- 2 tablespoons (30 ml) olive oil
- 1 tablespoon (15 ml) lemon juice
- Salt and pepper to taste

Instructions:

1. Heat olive oil in a skillet over medium heat.
2. Add grated cauliflower and cook for 5 minutes until tender.

3. In a large bowl, combine cauliflower, cherry tomatoes, cucumber, red onion, and parsley.
4. Drizzle with lemon juice and remaining olive oil.
5. Season with salt and pepper.
6. Toss gently and serve.

27. Spinach and Strawberry Salad

A sweet and savory salad that's perfect for a light lunch.

Servings: 2
Preparation Time: 10 minutes
Cooking Time: None
Ingredients:

- 2 cups (60 g) fresh spinach
- 1 cup (150 g) strawberries, sliced
- 1/4 cup (30 g) crumbled feta cheese
- 1/4 cup (30 g) sliced almonds
- 2 tablespoons (30 ml) balsamic vinaigrette

Instructions:

1. In a large bowl, combine spinach, strawberries, feta cheese, and almonds.
2. Drizzle with balsamic vinaigrette.
3. Toss gently and serve immediately.

28. Chickpea and Kale Soup

A hearty and nutritious soup that's perfect for lunch.

Servings: 4
Preparation Time: 15 minutes
Cooking Time: 30 minutes
Ingredients:

- 1 can (400 g) chickpeas, drained and rinsed
- 1 bunch kale, chopped
- 1 onion, diced
- 2 carrots, sliced
- 2 garlic cloves, minced
- 4 cups (1 liter) vegetable broth
- 1 can (400 g) diced tomatoes
- 1 teaspoon (5 g) thyme
- 1 teaspoon (5 g) rosemary
- Salt and pepper to taste

Instructions:

1. In a large pot, sauté onion, carrots, and garlic until softened.
2. Add chickpeas, kale, vegetable broth, diced tomatoes, thyme, and rosemary.
3. Bring to a boil, then reduce heat and simmer for 30 minutes.
4. Season with salt and pepper.
5. Serve hot.

29. Tuna Salad Lettuce Wraps

A low-carb and refreshing alternative to traditional tuna salad sandwiches.

Servings: 2
Preparation Time: 10 minutes
Cooking Time: None
Ingredients:

- 1 can (150 g) tuna in water, drained
- 1/4 cup (60 g) Greek yogurt
- 1 celery stalk, diced
- 1/4 cup (30 g) red onion, diced
- 1 tablespoon (15 ml) lemon juice
- Salt and pepper to taste
- 4 large lettuce leaves

Instructions:

1. In a bowl, mix tuna, Greek yogurt, celery, red onion, lemon juice, salt, and pepper.
2. Spoon mixture into lettuce leaves.
3. Roll up and serve immediately.

30. Roasted Veggie Wrap

A flavorful wrap filled with roasted vegetables and hummus.

Servings: 2
Preparation Time: 15 minutes
Cooking Time: 20 minutes

Ingredients:

- 1 zucchini, sliced
- 1 bell pepper, sliced
- 1 red onion, sliced

- 1 tablespoon (15 ml) olive oil
- Salt and pepper to taste
- 2 whole grain tortillas
- 1/2 cup (120 g) hummus

Instructions:

1. Preheat oven to 400°F (200°C).
2. Toss zucchini, bell pepper, and red onion with olive oil, salt, and pepper.
3. Spread the vegetables on a baking sheet and roast for 20 minutes until tender.
4. Spread hummus on each tortilla, add the roasted vegetables, and wrap tightly.
5. Slice in half and serve.

31. Thai Chicken Salad

A flavorful and vibrant salad with a Thai-inspired dressing.

Servings: 2
Preparation Time: 15 minutes
Cooking Time: 10 minutes
Ingredients:

- 1 grilled chicken breast, sliced
- 2 cups (60 g) mixed greens
- 1/2 cup (75 g) shredded carrots
- 1/4 cup (30 g) chopped peanuts
- 1/2 cup (75 g) red bell pepper, sliced
- 2 tablespoons (30 ml) lime juice
- 2 tablespoons (30 ml) fish sauce
- 1 tablespoon (15 ml) soy sauce
- 1 tablespoon (15 ml) honey
- 1 teaspoon (5 g) chili flakes

Instructions:

1. Arrange mixed greens on a plate.
2. Top with grilled chicken, carrots, peanuts, and red bell pepper.
3. In a small bowl, mix lime juice, fish sauce, soy sauce, honey, and chili flakes.
4. Drizzle the dressing over the salad.
5. Toss gently and serve immediately.

32. Zucchini Noodles with Pesto

A light and refreshing dish perfect for a quick lunch.

Servings: 2
Preparation Time: 10 minutes
Cooking Time: 5 minutes
Ingredients:

- 2 medium zucchinis, spiralized into noodles
- 1/4 cup (60 ml) pesto sauce
- 1/2 cup (75 g) cherry tomatoes, halved
- 1/4 cup (30 g) grated Parmesan cheese
- Salt and pepper to taste

Instructions:

1. Heat a skillet over medium heat and add the zucchini noodles.
2. Cook for 2-3 minutes until slightly tender.
3. Remove from heat and toss with pesto sauce.
4. Add cherry tomatoes and Parmesan cheese.
5. Season with salt and pepper.
6. Serve immediately.

33. Mediterranean Bowl

A hearty and nutritious bowl with Mediterranean flavors.

Servings: 2
Preparation Time: 15 minutes
Cooking Time: None
Ingredients:

- 1 cup (185 g) cooked quinoa
- 1/2 cup (75 g) cherry tomatoes, halved
- 1/2 cup (75 g) cucumber, diced
- 1/4 cup (30 g) Kalamata olives, sliced
- 1/4 cup (30 g) feta cheese, crumbled
- 1/4 cup (30 g) red onion, diced
- 2 tablespoons (30 ml) olive oil
- 1 tablespoon (15 ml) lemon juice
- Salt and pepper to taste

Instructions:

1. In a large bowl, combine quinoa, cherry tomatoes, cucumber, olives, feta cheese, and red onion.
2. Drizzle with olive oil and lemon juice.

3. Toss gently and season with salt and pepper.
4. Serve immediately.

34. Sweet Potato and Black Bean Chili
A flavorful and filling chili that's perfect for lunch.
Servings: 4
Preparation Time: 15 minutes
Cooking Time: 30 minutes
Ingredients:
- 1 large sweet potato, peeled and diced
- 1 can (400 g) black beans, drained and rinsed
- 1 can (400 g) diced tomatoes
- 1 onion, diced
- 2 garlic cloves, minced
- 1 tablespoon (15 ml) olive oil
- 1 teaspoon (5 g) cumin
- 1 teaspoon (5 g) chili powder
- 4 cups (1 liter) vegetable broth
- Salt and pepper to taste

Instructions:
1. In a large pot, heat olive oil over medium heat.
2. Add onion and garlic, sauté until softened.
3. Add sweet potato, cumin, and chili powder, and cook for 5 minutes.
4. Add black beans, diced tomatoes, and vegetable broth.
5. Bring to a boil, then reduce heat and simmer for 20-25 minutes until sweet potatoes are tender.
6. Season with salt and pepper.
7. Serve hot.

35. Eggplant Roll-Ups
Delicious and healthy roll-ups perfect for a light lunch.
Servings: 4
Preparation Time: 15 minutes
Cooking Time: 20 minutes

Ingredients:
- 1 large eggplant, thinly sliced lengthwise
- 1/2 cup (120 g) ricotta cheese
- 1/4 cup (30 g) Parmesan cheese, grated
- 1/4 cup (30 g) fresh basil, chopped
- 1 cup (240 ml) marinara sauce
- 1 tablespoon (15 ml) olive oil
- Salt and pepper to taste

Instructions:
1. Preheat oven to 375°F (190°C).
2. Brush eggplant slices with olive oil and season with salt and pepper.
3. Grill or bake eggplant slices until tender.
4. In a bowl, mix ricotta, Parmesan, and basil.
5. Place a spoonful of the cheese mixture on each eggplant slice and roll up.
6. Spread marinara sauce in a baking dish and place roll-ups on top.
7. Bake for 15-20 minutes until heated through.
8. Serve hot.

36. Shrimp and Avocado Salad
A light and refreshing salad with a zesty lime dressing.
Servings: 2
Preparation Time: 10 minutes
Cooking Time: 5 minutes
Ingredients:
- 1/2 pound (225 g) cooked shrimp
- 1 avocado, diced
- 1/2 cup (75 g) cherry tomatoes, halved
- 1/4 cup (30 g) red onion, diced
- 2 tablespoons (30 ml) lime juice
- 1 tablespoon (15 ml) olive oil
- Salt and pepper to taste

Instructions:
1. In a large bowl, combine shrimp, avocado, cherry tomatoes, and red onion.
2. Drizzle with lime juice and olive oil.
3. Toss gently and season with salt and pepper.

4. Serve immediately.

37. Broccoli and Cheese Soup

A creamy and comforting soup that's easy to make.

Servings: 4
Preparation Time: 15 minutes
Cooking Time: 20 minutes
Ingredients:

- 2 cups (300 g) broccoli florets
- 1 onion, diced
- 2 garlic cloves, minced
- 2 cups (480 ml) vegetable broth
- 1 cup (240 ml) unsweetened almond milk
- 1 cup (100 g) shredded cheddar cheese
- 1 tablespoon (15 ml) olive oil
- Salt and pepper to taste

Instructions:

1. In a large pot, heat olive oil over medium heat.
2. Add onion and garlic, sauté until softened.
3. Add broccoli florets and vegetable broth, bring to a boil.
4. Reduce heat and simmer until broccoli is tender, about 10 minutes.
5. Blend soup until smooth, then return to pot.
6. Stir in almond milk and cheddar cheese until melted.
7. Season with salt and pepper.
8. Serve hot.

38. Falafel Wrap

A delicious wrap filled with homemade falafel and fresh veggies.

Servings: 2
Preparation Time: 15 minutes
Cooking Time: 10 minutes
Ingredients:

- 1 cup (200 g) canned chickpeas, drained and rinsed
- 1/4 cup (30 g) onion, chopped
- 2 garlic cloves
- 1/4 cup (30 g) fresh parsley
- 1 teaspoon (5 g) cumin
- 1 teaspoon (5 g) coriander
- 1 tablespoon (15 ml) lemon juice
- Salt and pepper to taste
- 2 whole grain tortillas
- 1/2 cup (120 g) hummus
- 1/2 cup (75 g) chopped cucumber
- 1/2 cup (75 g) chopped tomatoes

Instructions:

1. In a food processor, combine chickpeas, onion, garlic, parsley, cumin, coriander, lemon juice, salt, and pepper. Process until smooth.
2. Form mixture into small patties.
3. Heat olive oil in a skillet over medium heat and cook falafel patties until golden brown on both sides.
4. Spread hummus on tortillas, add falafel patties, and top with chopped cucumber and tomatoes.
5. Roll up the tortillas, slice in half, and serve.

39. Spaghetti Squash Bowl

A light and low-carb alternative to traditional pasta dishes.

Servings: 2
Preparation Time: 10 minutes
Cooking Time: 40 minutes
Ingredients:

- 1 spaghetti squash
- 1 cup (240 ml) marinara sauce
- 1/2 cup (75 g) cherry tomatoes, halved
- 1/4 cup (30 g) Parmesan cheese, grated
- 2 tablespoons (30 ml) olive oil
- Salt and pepper to taste

Instructions:

1. Preheat oven to 400°F (200°C).
2. Cut the spaghetti squash in half lengthwise and remove the seeds.

3. Drizzle with olive oil, season with salt and pepper, and place cut-side down on a baking sheet.
4. Roast for 40 minutes or until tender.
5. Use a fork to scrape out the spaghetti-like strands.
6. In a bowl, combine the spaghetti squash with marinara sauce, cherry tomatoes, and Parmesan cheese.
7. Toss gently and serve immediately.

40. Greek Salad with Grilled Fish

A fresh and healthy salad paired with perfectly grilled fish.

Servings: 2
Preparation Time: 15 minutes
Cooking Time: 10 minutes
Ingredients:

- 2 fish fillets (such as tilapia or salmon)
- 2 cups (60 g) mixed greens
- 1/2 cup (75 g) cherry tomatoes, halved
- 1/4 cup (30 g) cucumber, sliced
- 1/4 cup (30 g) red onion, thinly sliced
- 1/4 cup (30 g) Kalamata olives, pitted and sliced
- 1/4 cup (30 g) feta cheese, crumbled
- 2 tablespoons (30 ml) olive oil
- 1 tablespoon (15 ml) lemon juice
- 1 teaspoon (5 g) dried oregano
- Salt and pepper to taste

Instructions:

1. Preheat a grill or grill pan over medium-high heat.
2. Season the fish fillets with salt, pepper, and dried oregano.
3. Grill the fish for 4-5 minutes on each side or until fully cooked.
4. In a large bowl, combine mixed greens, cherry tomatoes, cucumber, red onion, olives, and feta cheese.
5. Drizzle with olive oil and lemon juice.
6. Toss gently and serve the salad topped with the grilled fish.

Chapter 8: Satisfying Snacks

Snacks can be an important part of a balanced diet, especially for those managing diabetes. Choosing the right snacks can help maintain energy levels, keep blood sugar stable, and prevent overeating at meal times. This chapter offers a variety of delicious and healthy snack options that are easy to prepare and perfect for curbing hunger between meals.

41. Apple Slices with Almond Butter
A simple and nutritious snack that combines the fiber of apples with the protein and healthy fats of almond butter.
Servings: 1
Preparation Time: 5 minutes
Cooking Time: None
Ingredients:
- 1 apple, sliced
- 2 tablespoons (30 g) almond butter

Instructions:
1. Wash and slice the apple.
2. Serve apple slices with almond butter on the side for dipping.
3. Enjoy immediately.

42. Hummus and Veggie Sticks
A crunchy and satisfying snack that's full of fiber and protein.
Servings: 2
Preparation Time: 10 minutes
Cooking Time: None
Ingredients:
- 1 cup (240 g) hummus
- 1 carrot, cut into sticks
- 1 cucumber, cut into sticks
- 1 bell pepper, cut into sticks
- 1 celery stalk, cut into sticks

Instructions:
1. Arrange the vegetable sticks on a plate.
2. Serve with a bowl of hummus for dipping.
3. Enjoy immediately.

43. Greek Yogurt with Nuts
A creamy and crunchy snack that's rich in protein and healthy fats.
Servings: 1
Preparation Time: 5 minutes
Cooking Time: None
Ingredients:
- 1 cup (240 ml) plain Greek yogurt
- 2 tablespoons (30 g) mixed nuts (almonds, walnuts, pecans)
- 1 teaspoon (5 ml) honey (optional)

Instructions:
1. Scoop Greek yogurt into a bowl.
2. Top with mixed nuts.
3. Drizzle with honey if desired.
4. Enjoy immediately.

44. Roasted Chickpeas
A crunchy and savory snack that's high in fiber and protein.
Servings: 4
Preparation Time: 10 minutes
Cooking Time: 30 minutes
Ingredients:
- 1 can (400 g) chickpeas, drained and rinsed
- 1 tablespoon (15 ml) olive oil
- 1 teaspoon (5 g) paprika
- 1/2 teaspoon (2.5 g) garlic powder
- Salt to taste

Instructions:
1. Preheat oven to 400°F (200°C).
2. Toss chickpeas with olive oil, paprika, garlic powder, and salt.

3. Spread chickpeas on a baking sheet in a single layer.
4. Roast for 30 minutes, stirring halfway through, until crispy.
5. Let cool and enjoy.

45. Cottage Cheese and Pineapple

A refreshing and protein-rich snack with a hint of sweetness.

Servings: 1
Preparation Time: 5 minutes
Cooking Time: None
Ingredients:

- 1 cup (240 g) cottage cheese
- 1/2 cup (75 g) pineapple chunks (fresh or canned in juice)

Instructions:

1. Scoop cottage cheese into a bowl.
2. Top with pineapple chunks.
3. Enjoy immediately.

46. Mixed Nuts and Seeds

A nutrient-dense snack that's easy to take on the go.

Servings: 1
Preparation Time: 5 minutes
Cooking Time: None
Ingredients:

- 1/4 cup (30 g) mixed nuts (almonds, walnuts, cashews)
- 2 tablespoons (20 g) mixed seeds (sunflower, pumpkin, chia)

Instructions:

1. Combine mixed nuts and seeds in a small bowl or container.
2. Enjoy immediately or take with you for a snack later.

47. Avocado and Tomato Slices

A simple and delicious snack that's full of healthy fats and fiber.

Servings: 1
Preparation Time: 5 minutes
Cooking Time: None
Ingredients:

- 1 avocado, sliced
- 1 tomato, sliced
- Salt and pepper to taste

Instructions:

1. Arrange avocado and tomato slices on a plate.
2. Season with salt and pepper.
3. Enjoy immediately.

48. Berry and Nut Mix

A sweet and crunchy snack that's rich in antioxidants and healthy fats.

Servings: 1
Preparation Time: 5 minutes
Cooking Time: None
Ingredients:

- 1/4 cup (35 g) mixed berries (blueberries, raspberries, strawberries)
- 2 tablespoons (30 g) mixed nuts (almonds, walnuts, pecans)

Instructions:

1. Combine mixed berries and nuts in a small bowl.
2. Enjoy immediately.

49. Cheese and Whole Grain Crackers

A satisfying and balanced snack with protein and fiber.

Servings: 1
Preparation Time: 5 minutes
Cooking Time: None
Ingredients:

- 1 ounce (28 g) cheese (cheddar, mozzarella, Swiss)
- 6 whole grain crackers

Instructions:

1. Slice cheese into small pieces.
2. Arrange cheese and crackers on a plate.
3. Enjoy immediately.

50. Veggie Chips

A crunchy and healthy alternative to traditional potato chips.

Servings: 4
Preparation Time: 10 minutes
Cooking Time: 30 minutes
Ingredients:

- 1 zucchini, thinly sliced
- 1 sweet potato, thinly sliced
- 1 beet, thinly sliced
- 1 tablespoon (15 ml) olive oil
- Salt to taste

Instructions:

1. Preheat oven to 375°F (190°C).
2. Toss vegetable slices with olive oil and salt.
3. Spread slices on a baking sheet in a single layer.
4. Bake for 20-30 minutes, turning halfway through, until crispy.
5. Let cool and enjoy.

51. Protein Balls

A nutritious and energy-boosting snack that's easy to prepare and perfect for on-the-go.

Servings: 12 balls
Preparation Time: 10 minutes
Cooking Time: None
Ingredients:

- 1 cup (90 g) rolled oats
- 1/2 cup (125 g) peanut butter or almond butter
- 1/4 cup (85 g) honey or maple syrup
- 1/4 cup (30 g) chocolate chips or cacao nibs
- 1/4 cup (30 g) flaxseed meal

Instructions:

1. In a large bowl, combine all ingredients and mix well.
2. Roll the mixture into 1-inch balls.
3. Refrigerate for at least 30 minutes before serving.

4. Store in an airtight container in the refrigerator.

52. Edamame

A simple and protein-rich snack that's perfect for satisfying hunger.

Servings: 2
Preparation Time: 5 minutes
Cooking Time: 5 minutes
Ingredients:

- 2 cups (300 g) edamame (fresh or frozen)
- Salt to taste

Instructions:

1. Boil or steam edamame for 5 minutes until tender.
2. Drain and sprinkle with salt.
3. Serve warm or chilled.

53. Celery with Peanut Butter

A crunchy and satisfying snack that combines fiber and protein.

Servings: 1
Preparation Time: 5 minutes
Cooking Time: None
Ingredients:

- 2 celery stalks, cut into sticks
- 2 tablespoons (30 g) peanut butter

Instructions:

1. Spread peanut butter inside the celery sticks.
2. Enjoy immediately.

54. Dark Chocolate Squares

A sweet and indulgent treat that can be enjoyed in moderation.

Servings: 1
Preparation Time: None
Cooking Time: None
Ingredients:

- 2 squares (20 g) dark chocolate (70% cocoa or higher)

Instructions:

1. Enjoy dark chocolate squares as a satisfying snack.

55. Smoked Salmon on Cucumber Slices

A light and elegant snack that's rich in healthy fats and protein.

Servings: 2
Preparation Time: 10 minutes
Cooking Time: None
Ingredients:

- 1 cucumber, sliced
- 4 ounces (115 g) smoked salmon
- 1 tablespoon (15 g) cream cheese
- Fresh dill for garnish

Instructions:

1. Spread a small amount of cream cheese on each cucumber slice.
2. Top with a piece of smoked salmon.
3. Garnish with fresh dill.
4. Serve immediately.

56. Hard-Boiled Eggs

A classic and protein-packed snack that's easy to prepare.

Servings: 2
Preparation Time: 5 minutes
Cooking Time: 10 minutes
Ingredients:

- 4 large eggs
- Salt and pepper to taste

Instructions:

1. Place eggs in a pot and cover with water.
2. Bring to a boil, then reduce heat and simmer for 10 minutes.
3. Drain and cool eggs under cold water.
4. Peel and slice eggs, and season with salt and pepper.

57. Guacamole and Veggie Dippers

A tasty and healthy snack full of healthy fats and fiber.

Servings: 2
Preparation Time: 10 minutes
Cooking Time: None
Ingredients:

- 2 ripe avocados
- 1 small tomato, diced
- 1/4 cup (30 g) red onion, diced
- 1 tablespoon (15 ml) lime juice
- Salt and pepper to taste
- Veggie sticks (carrots, celery, bell peppers) for dipping

Instructions:

1. Mash avocados in a bowl.
2. Stir in tomato, red onion, lime juice, salt, and pepper.
3. Serve with veggie sticks.

58. Fresh Fruit Salad

A refreshing and naturally sweet snack that's full of vitamins.

Servings: 2
Preparation Time: 10 minutes
Cooking Time: None
Ingredients:

- 1 cup (150 g) mixed berries (strawberries, blueberries, raspberries)
- 1 apple, diced
- 1 banana, sliced
- 1 orange, segmented
- 1 tablespoon (15 ml) lemon juice

Instructions:

1. Combine all fruits in a large bowl.
2. Drizzle with lemon juice and toss gently.
3. Serve immediately.

59. Almond Flour Crackers

A crunchy and low-carb alternative to traditional crackers.

Servings: 4
Preparation Time: 15 minutes
Cooking Time: 15 minutes
Ingredients:

- 1 cup (120 g) almond flour

- 1 egg
- 1/4 teaspoon (1.25 g) salt
- 1/4 teaspoon (1.25 g) garlic powder

Instructions:
1. Preheat oven to 350°F (175°C).
2. In a bowl, mix almond flour, egg, salt, and garlic powder until a dough forms.
3. Roll out the dough between two sheets of parchment paper to 1/8 inch thickness.
4. Cut into squares and place on a baking sheet.
5. Bake for 12-15 minutes until golden brown.
6. Let cool and serve.

60. Popcorn

A light and crunchy snack that's high in fiber.

Servings: 2
Preparation Time: 5 minutes
Cooking Time: 5 minutes
Ingredients:
- 1/4 cup (50 g) popcorn kernels
- 1 tablespoon (15 ml) olive oil
- Salt to taste

Instructions:
1. Heat olive oil in a large pot over medium heat.
2. Add popcorn kernels and cover the pot.
3. Shake the pot occasionally until popping slows.
4. Remove from heat and season with salt.
5. Serve immediately.

Chapter 9: Hearty Dinners

Dinner is often the main meal of the day, providing a chance to refuel and unwind. For those managing diabetes, it's essential to focus on balanced, nutritious meals that support overall health and maintain stable blood sugar levels. This chapter offers a variety of hearty, satisfying dinner recipes that are both delicious and diabetes-friendly.

61. Baked Salmon with Asparagus

A simple and nutritious meal featuring omega-3 rich salmon and fiber-packed asparagus.

Servings: 2
Preparation Time: 10 minutes
Cooking Time: 20 minutes
Ingredients:
- 2 salmon fillets
- 1 bunch asparagus, trimmed
- 2 tablespoons (30 ml) olive oil
- 1 lemon, sliced
- Salt and pepper to taste

Instructions:
1. Preheat the oven to 400°F (200°C).
2. Place salmon fillets and asparagus on a baking sheet.
3. Drizzle with olive oil and season with salt and pepper.
4. Arrange lemon slices over the salmon.
5. Bake for 20 minutes or until the salmon is cooked through and the asparagus is tender.
6. Serve immediately.

62. Chicken and Veggie Stir-Fry

A quick and versatile stir-fry packed with lean protein and fresh vegetables.

Servings: 2
Preparation Time: 10 minutes
Cooking Time: 15 minutes
Ingredients:
- 2 chicken breasts, thinly sliced
- 1 cup (150 g) broccoli florets
- 1 red bell pepper, sliced
- 1 carrot, sliced
- 1 zucchini, sliced
- 2 tablespoons (30 ml) soy sauce
- 1 tablespoon (15 ml) sesame oil
- 1 tablespoon (15 ml) olive oil
- 1 garlic clove, minced
- 1 teaspoon (5 g) ginger, minced

Instructions:
1. Heat olive oil in a large skillet over medium-high heat.
2. Add garlic and ginger, sauté for 1 minute.
3. Add chicken slices and cook until browned.
4. Add broccoli, bell pepper, carrot, and zucchini.
5. Stir-fry for 5-7 minutes until vegetables are tender.
6. Add soy sauce and sesame oil, stir to combine.
7. Serve hot.

63. Beef and Broccoli

A classic and hearty dish that's both flavorful and nutritious.

Servings: 2
Preparation Time: 10 minutes
Cooking Time: 15 minutes
Ingredients:
- 1/2 pound (225 g) beef sirloin, thinly sliced
- 2 cups (300 g) broccoli florets
- 1/4 cup (60 ml) soy sauce
- 2 tablespoons (30 ml) oyster sauce
- 1 tablespoon (15 ml) olive oil
- 1 garlic clove, minced
- 1 teaspoon (5 g) ginger, minced

Instructions:

1. Heat olive oil in a large skillet over medium-high heat.
2. Add garlic and ginger, sauté for 1 minute.
3. Add beef slices and cook until browned.
4. Add broccoli florets and cook for another 5 minutes.
5. Stir in soy sauce and oyster sauce.
6. Cook for another 3 minutes until broccoli is tender.
7. Serve hot.

64. Zucchini Lasagna

A low-carb lasagna that's packed with vegetables and flavor.

Servings: 4
Preparation Time: 20 minutes
Cooking Time: 40 minutes
Ingredients:

- 3 large zucchinis, sliced lengthwise into thin strips
- 1 pound (450 g) ground turkey
- 2 cups (480 ml) marinara sauce
- 1 cup (240 g) ricotta cheese
- 1 cup (100 g) shredded mozzarella cheese
- 1/4 cup (25 g) grated Parmesan cheese
- 1 egg
- 1 tablespoon (15 ml) olive oil
- 1 teaspoon (5 g) Italian seasoning
- Salt and pepper to taste

Instructions:

1. Preheat oven to 375°F (190°C).
2. Heat olive oil in a skillet and cook ground turkey until browned.
3. Add marinara sauce and Italian seasoning, simmer for 10 minutes.
4. In a bowl, mix ricotta cheese, egg, and Parmesan cheese.
5. In a baking dish, layer zucchini slices, turkey mixture, ricotta mixture, and mozzarella cheese.
6. Repeat layers and top with remaining mozzarella.
7. Bake for 40 minutes or until bubbly and golden.
8. Let cool for 10 minutes before serving.

65. Stuffed Bell Peppers

Bell peppers stuffed with a delicious mixture of ground meat, rice, and vegetables.

Servings: 4
Preparation Time: 15 minutes
Cooking Time: 40 minutes
Ingredients:

- 4 large bell peppers, tops cut off and seeds removed
- 1/2 pound (225 g) ground beef or turkey
- 1 cup (185 g) cooked brown rice
- 1 can (400 g) diced tomatoes
- 1/2 cup (75 g) diced onion
- 1/2 cup (75 g) diced zucchini
- 1/2 cup (60 g) shredded cheese
- 1 tablespoon (15 ml) olive oil
- Salt and pepper to taste

Instructions:

1. Preheat oven to 375°F (190°C).
2. Heat olive oil in a skillet and cook ground meat until browned.
3. Add onion and zucchini, cook until softened.
4. Stir in diced tomatoes and cooked rice, season with salt and pepper.
5. Stuff the bell peppers with the mixture and place in a baking dish.
6. Top with shredded cheese.
7. Bake for 40 minutes or until peppers are tender and cheese is melted.
8. Serve hot.

66. Pork Tenderloin with Brussels Sprouts

A savory and satisfying dish featuring tender pork and roasted Brussels sprouts.

Servings: 4
Preparation Time: 10 minutes
Cooking Time: 25 minutes
Ingredients:

- 1 pound (450 g) pork tenderloin
- 1 pound (450 g) Brussels sprouts, halved
- 2 tablespoons (30 ml) olive oil
- 1 tablespoon (15 ml) Dijon mustard
- 1 teaspoon (5 g) garlic powder
- 1 teaspoon (5 g) paprika
- Salt and pepper to taste

Instructions:

1. Preheat oven to 400°F (200°C).
2. Rub pork tenderloin with Dijon mustard, garlic powder, paprika, salt, and pepper.
3. Toss Brussels sprouts with olive oil, salt, and pepper.
4. Place pork and Brussels sprouts on a baking sheet.
5. Roast for 25 minutes or until pork is cooked through and Brussels sprouts are tender.
6. Let pork rest for 5 minutes before slicing.
7. Serve with Brussels sprouts.

67. Quinoa-Stuffed Squash

A wholesome and flavorful dish featuring nutrient-rich quinoa and roasted squash.

Servings: 4
Preparation Time: 15 minutes
Cooking Time: 40 minutes
Ingredients:

- 2 acorn squash, halved and seeds removed
- 1 cup (185 g) cooked quinoa
- 1/2 cup (75 g) diced red bell pepper
- 1/4 cup (30 g) diced red onion
- 1/4 cup (30 g) dried cranberries
- 1/4 cup (30 g) chopped pecans
- 1 tablespoon (15 ml) olive oil
- 1 teaspoon (5 g) cinnamon
- Salt and pepper to taste

Instructions:

1. Preheat oven to 400°F (200°C).
2. Brush squash halves with olive oil and season with salt and pepper.
3. Place squash cut-side down on a baking sheet and roast for 30 minutes.
4. In a bowl, combine cooked quinoa, red bell pepper, red onion, dried cranberries, chopped pecans, olive oil, cinnamon, salt, and pepper.
5. Remove squash from oven, flip over, and stuff with quinoa mixture.
6. Return to oven and bake for an additional 10 minutes.
7. Serve immediately.

68. Lemon Garlic Shrimp

A light and zesty dish that's quick to prepare and bursting with flavor.

Servings: 2
Preparation Time: 10 minutes
Cooking Time: 10 minutes
Ingredients:

- 1/2 pound (225 g) shrimp, peeled and deveined
- 2 tablespoons (30 ml) olive oil
- 2 garlic cloves, minced
- 1 lemon, juiced and zested
- 1/4 cup (30 g) chopped parsley
- Salt and pepper to taste

Instructions:

1. Heat olive oil in a large skillet over medium heat.
2. Add garlic and sauté for 1 minute.
3. Add shrimp, lemon juice, lemon zest, salt, and pepper.
4. Cook for 3-4 minutes until shrimp are pink and opaque.
5. Stir in chopped parsley.
6. Serve immediately.

69. Turkey Meatballs with Spaghetti Squash

A low-carb twist on a classic comfort food.

Servings: 4
Preparation Time: 20 minutes
Cooking Time: 40 minutes
Ingredients:

- 1 pound (450 g) ground turkey
- 1/4 cup (30 g) breadcrumbs
- 1/4 cup (30 g) grated Parmesan cheese
- 1 egg
- 1 teaspoon (5 g) Italian seasoning
- Salt and pepper to taste
- 1 spaghetti squash
- 2 cups (480 ml) marinara sauce
- 2 tablespoons (30 ml) olive oil

Instructions:

1. Preheat the oven to 375°F (190°C).
2. Cut the spaghetti squash in half, remove the seeds, and drizzle with olive oil. Place cut-side down on a baking sheet and bake for 40 minutes.
3. In a bowl, mix ground turkey, breadcrumbs, Parmesan cheese, egg, Italian seasoning, salt, and pepper. Form into meatballs.
4. Heat olive oil in a skillet over medium heat and cook the meatballs until browned and cooked through.
5. Heat marinara sauce in a saucepan and add the cooked meatballs.
6. Use a fork to scrape the spaghetti squash into strands.
7. Serve meatballs over spaghetti squash and top with extra sauce.

70. Grilled Veggie Skewers

A colorful and nutritious dish perfect for a summer evening.

Servings: 4
Preparation Time: 15 minutes
Cooking Time: 10 minutes
Ingredients:

- 1 zucchini, sliced
- 1 yellow squash, sliced
- 1 red bell pepper, cut into chunks
- 1 red onion, cut into chunks
- 1 cup (150 g) cherry tomatoes
- 2 tablespoons (30 ml) olive oil
- 1 teaspoon (5 g) garlic powder
- Salt and pepper to taste
- Wooden or metal skewers

Instructions:

1. Preheat the grill to medium-high heat.
2. Thread the vegetables onto the skewers.
3. In a small bowl, mix olive oil, garlic powder, salt, and pepper. Brush the mixture onto the vegetables.
4. Grill the skewers for about 10 minutes, turning occasionally, until vegetables are tender and lightly charred.
5. Serve immediately.

71. Cauliflower Crust Pizza

A low-carb alternative to traditional pizza that's both delicious and healthy.

Servings: 4
Preparation Time: 20 minutes
Cooking Time: 25 minutes
Ingredients:

- 1 head of cauliflower, riced
- 1/2 cup (50 g) shredded mozzarella cheese
- 1/4 cup (25 g) grated Parmesan cheese
- 1 egg
- 1 teaspoon (5 g) Italian seasoning
- Salt and pepper to taste
- 1/2 cup (120 ml) marinara sauce
- 1 cup (100 g) shredded mozzarella cheese for topping
- Your favorite pizza toppings (e.g., bell peppers, mushrooms, onions, olives)

Instructions:

1. Preheat oven to 425°F (220°C).
2. Microwave riced cauliflower for 4-5 minutes until soft. Let cool, then squeeze out excess moisture using a clean towel.

3. In a bowl, combine cauliflower, mozzarella, Parmesan, egg, Italian seasoning, salt, and pepper. Mix well.
4. Press the mixture onto a parchment-lined baking sheet to form a crust.
5. Bake for 15 minutes until golden brown.
6. Remove from oven, spread marinara sauce on top, and add shredded cheese and your favorite toppings.
7. Bake for an additional 10 minutes until cheese is melted and bubbly.
8. Serve hot.

72. Chicken Fajita Bowl

A flavorful and satisfying bowl that's easy to customize.

Servings: 4
Preparation Time: 15 minutes
Cooking Time: 15 minutes
Ingredients:

- 2 chicken breasts, sliced
- 1 red bell pepper, sliced
- 1 green bell pepper, sliced
- 1 onion, sliced
- 2 tablespoons (30 ml) olive oil
- 1 teaspoon (5 g) chili powder
- 1 teaspoon (5 g) cumin
- 1 teaspoon (5 g) paprika
- Salt and pepper to taste
- 2 cups (370 g) cooked brown rice
- 1 avocado, sliced
- 1/4 cup (60 g) salsa
- Fresh cilantro for garnish

Instructions:

1. Heat olive oil in a skillet over medium-high heat.
2. Add chicken slices and cook until browned.
3. Add bell peppers, onion, chili powder, cumin, paprika, salt, and pepper. Cook until vegetables are tender.
4. Serve chicken and vegetables over brown rice.

5. Top with avocado slices, salsa, and fresh cilantro.
6. Serve immediately.

73. Baked Cod with Green Beans

A light and healthy meal that's quick and easy to prepare.

Servings: 2
Preparation Time: 10 minutes
Cooking Time: 20 minutes
Ingredients:

- 2 cod fillets
- 1/2 pound (225 g) green beans, trimmed
- 2 tablespoons (30 ml) olive oil
- 1 lemon, sliced
- 1 teaspoon (5 g) garlic powder
- Salt and pepper to taste

Instructions:

1. Preheat oven to 400°F (200°C).
2. Place cod fillets and green beans on a baking sheet.
3. Drizzle with olive oil and season with garlic powder, salt, and pepper.
4. Arrange lemon slices over the cod.
5. Bake for 20 minutes or until cod is cooked through and green beans are tender.
6. Serve immediately.

74. Eggplant Parmesan

A healthier version of the classic Italian dish that's baked instead of fried.

Servings: 4
Preparation Time: 20 minutes
Cooking Time: 30 minutes
Ingredients:

- 2 large eggplants, sliced into rounds
- 2 cups (480 ml) marinara sauce
- 1 cup (100 g) shredded mozzarella cheese
- 1/2 cup (50 g) grated Parmesan cheese
- 1/2 cup (60 g) whole wheat breadcrumbs
- 1 egg, beaten
- 2 tablespoons (30 ml) olive oil

- Salt and pepper to taste

Instructions:
1. Preheat oven to 375°F (190°C).
2. Dip eggplant slices in beaten egg, then coat with breadcrumbs.
3. Arrange on a baking sheet and drizzle with olive oil.
4. Bake for 20 minutes until golden brown.
5. Spread a layer of marinara sauce in a baking dish, then add a layer of eggplant slices. Top with mozzarella and Parmesan cheese.
6. Repeat layers until all ingredients are used, ending with cheese on top.
7. Bake for an additional 10 minutes until cheese is melted and bubbly.
8. Serve hot.

75. Lentil and Veggie Stew
A hearty and nutritious stew that's perfect for a comforting dinner.
Servings: 4
Preparation Time: 15 minutes
Cooking Time: 40 minutes
Ingredients:
- 1 cup (200 g) dried lentils, rinsed
- 1 onion, diced
- 2 carrots, sliced
- 2 celery stalks, sliced
- 2 garlic cloves, minced
- 1 can (400 g) diced tomatoes
- 4 cups (1 liter) vegetable broth
- 1 teaspoon (5 g) cumin
- 1 teaspoon (5 g) thyme
- Salt and pepper to taste

Instructions:
1. In a large pot, sauté onion, carrots, celery, and garlic until softened.
2. Add lentils, diced tomatoes, vegetable broth, cumin, and thyme.
3. Bring to a boil, then reduce heat and simmer for 30-40 minutes until lentils are tender.

4. Season with salt and pepper.
5. Serve hot.

76. Grilled Chicken with Avocado Salsa
A flavorful and fresh dish that's perfect for a light dinner.
Servings: 2
Preparation Time: 10 minutes
Cooking Time: 15 minutes
Ingredients:
- 2 chicken breasts
- 1 tablespoon (15 ml) olive oil
- 1 teaspoon (5 g) garlic powder
- Salt and pepper to taste
- 1 avocado, diced
- 1 tomato, diced
- 1/4 cup (30 g) red onion, diced
- 1 tablespoon (15 ml) lime juice
- Fresh cilantro for garnish

Instructions:
1. Preheat grill to medium-high heat.
2. Rub chicken breasts with olive oil, garlic powder, salt, and pepper.
3. Grill chicken for 6-7 minutes on each side until fully cooked.
4. In a bowl, combine avocado, tomato, red onion, lime juice, and cilantro.
5. Serve grilled chicken topped with avocado salsa.

77. Herb-Crusted Tilapia
A light and flavorful fish dish that's easy to prepare and rich in protein.
Servings: 2
Preparation Time: 10 minutes
Cooking Time: 15 minutes
Ingredients:
- 2 tilapia fillets
- 1/4 cup (25 g) breadcrumbs
- 1/4 cup (30 g) grated Parmesan cheese
- 1 tablespoon (15 ml) olive oil
- 1 teaspoon (5 g) dried basil
- 1 teaspoon (5 g) dried oregano

- Salt and pepper to taste

Instructions:

1. Preheat oven to 400°F (200°C).
2. In a bowl, mix breadcrumbs, Parmesan cheese, basil, oregano, salt, and pepper.
3. Brush tilapia fillets with olive oil and coat with the breadcrumb mixture.
4. Place on a baking sheet and bake for 15 minutes or until the fish flakes easily with a fork.
5. Serve immediately.

78. Beef Stir-Fry with Snow Peas

A quick and delicious stir-fry that's packed with protein and fresh vegetables.

Servings: 2
Preparation Time: 10 minutes
Cooking Time: 15 minutes
Ingredients:

- 1/2 pound (225 g) beef sirloin, thinly sliced
- 1 cup (150 g) snow peas
- 1 red bell pepper, sliced
- 1 onion, sliced
- 2 tablespoons (30 ml) soy sauce
- 1 tablespoon (15 ml) sesame oil
- 1 tablespoon (15 ml) olive oil
- 1 garlic clove, minced
- 1 teaspoon (5 g) ginger, minced

Instructions:

1. Heat olive oil in a large skillet over medium-high heat.
2. Add garlic and ginger, sauté for 1 minute.
3. Add beef slices and cook until browned.
4. Add snow peas, bell pepper, and onion. Stir-fry for 5-7 minutes.
5. Add soy sauce and sesame oil, stir to combine.
6. Serve hot.

79. Stuffed Zucchini Boats

A healthy and satisfying dish that's perfect for a nutritious dinner.

Servings: 4
Preparation Time: 15 minutes
Cooking Time: 30 minutes
Ingredients:

- 4 zucchinis, halved lengthwise and seeds removed
- 1/2 pound (225 g) ground turkey
- 1/2 cup (75 g) diced tomatoes
- 1/4 cup (30 g) diced onion
- 1/4 cup (30 g) grated Parmesan cheese
- 1 tablespoon (15 ml) olive oil
- 1 teaspoon (5 g) Italian seasoning
- Salt and pepper to taste

Instructions:

1. Preheat oven to 375°F (190°C).
2. Heat olive oil in a skillet and cook ground turkey until browned.
3. Add diced tomatoes, onion, Italian seasoning, salt, and pepper. Cook for another 5 minutes.
4. Fill zucchini halves with the turkey mixture and place in a baking dish.
5. Sprinkle with Parmesan cheese.
6. Bake for 30 minutes or until zucchini is tender.
7. Serve hot.

80. Thai Red Curry

A flavorful and aromatic curry that's both satisfying and healthy.

Servings: 4
Preparation Time: 15 minutes
Cooking Time: 20 minutes
Ingredients:

- 1 pound (450 g) chicken breast, sliced
- 1 can (400 ml) coconut milk
- 2 tablespoons (30 g) red curry paste
- 1 red bell pepper, sliced
- 1 green bell pepper, sliced
- 1 onion, sliced

- 1 cup (150 g) snap peas
- 2 tablespoons (30 ml) fish sauce
- 1 tablespoon (15 ml) lime juice
- Fresh basil leaves for garnish

Instructions:

1. Heat a large skillet over medium heat and add red curry paste. Cook for 1 minute.
2. Add sliced chicken and cook until browned.
3. Stir in coconut milk, fish sauce, and lime juice.
4. Add bell peppers, onion, and snap peas. Simmer for 10 minutes until vegetables are tender.
5. Garnish with fresh basil leaves.
6. Serve hot over brown rice or cauliflower rice.

Chapter 10: Delectable Desserts

Managing diabetes doesn't mean you have to give up desserts. With a bit of creativity and the right ingredients, you can enjoy a variety of delicious and satisfying treats that fit into your meal plan. This chapter offers a selection of delectable, diabetes-friendly desserts that are both indulgent and nutritious.

81. Almond Flour Brownies

Rich and fudgy brownies made with almond flour, perfect for a guilt-free treat.

Servings: 12
Preparation Time: 10 minutes
Cooking Time: 25 minutes
Ingredients:

- 1 cup (100 g) almond flour
- 1/2 cup (50 g) cocoa powder
- 1/2 cup (100 g) coconut sugar or sugar substitute
- 1/4 cup (60 ml) melted coconut oil
- 2 large eggs
- 1 teaspoon (5 ml) vanilla extract
- 1/2 teaspoon (2.5 g) baking soda
- A pinch of salt

Instructions:

1. Preheat oven to 350°F (175°C).
2. In a bowl, mix almond flour, cocoa powder, coconut sugar, baking soda, and salt.
3. In another bowl, whisk together melted coconut oil, eggs, and vanilla extract.
4. Combine wet and dry ingredients, stirring until well mixed.
5. Pour the batter into a greased or lined baking dish.
6. Bake for 20-25 minutes, or until a toothpick inserted into the center comes out clean.
7. Let cool before slicing and serving.

82. Berry Chia Pudding

A creamy and nutrient-rich pudding that's perfect for a light dessert.

Servings: 4
Preparation Time: 10 minutes
Cooking Time: None (Refrigeration: 4 hours)
Ingredients:

- 1/4 cup (40 g) chia seeds
- 1 cup (240 ml) unsweetened almond milk
- 1/2 cup (75 g) mixed berries (fresh or frozen)
- 1 tablespoon (15 ml) maple syrup or sweetener of choice
- 1 teaspoon (5 ml) vanilla extract

Instructions:

1. In a bowl, mix chia seeds, almond milk, maple syrup, and vanilla extract.
2. Stir well and let sit for 5 minutes. Stir again to prevent clumping.
3. Cover and refrigerate for at least 4 hours or overnight.
4. Before serving, stir well and top with mixed berries.

83. Coconut Flour Cookies

Soft and chewy cookies that are low in carbs and high in flavor.

Servings: 12
Preparation Time: 10 minutes
Cooking Time: 15 minutes
Ingredients:

- 1/2 cup (60 g) coconut flour
- 1/4 cup (60 ml) coconut oil, melted
- 1/4 cup (50 g) coconut sugar or sugar substitute
- 2 large eggs
- 1 teaspoon (5 ml) vanilla extract
- 1/2 teaspoon (2.5 g) baking powder
- A pinch of salt

Instructions:

1. Preheat oven to 350°F (175°C).
2. In a bowl, mix coconut flour, coconut sugar, baking powder, and salt.
3. In another bowl, whisk together melted coconut oil, eggs, and vanilla extract.
4. Combine wet and dry ingredients, stirring until a dough forms.
5. Scoop dough onto a baking sheet, flattening slightly.
6. Bake for 12-15 minutes, or until edges are golden brown.
7. Let cool before serving.

84. Sugar-Free Cheesecake

A creamy and indulgent cheesecake that's free of added sugars.

Servings: 8
Preparation Time: 15 minutes
Cooking Time: 1 hour (plus chilling time)
Ingredients:

- 2 cups (200 g) almond flour
- 1/4 cup (60 g) melted butter
- 1/4 cup (50 g) erythritol or sugar substitute
- 16 ounces (450 g) cream cheese, softened
- 1/2 cup (100 g) erythritol or sugar substitute
- 3 large eggs
- 1 teaspoon (5 ml) vanilla extract
- 1/4 cup (60 ml) sour cream

Instructions:

1. Preheat oven to 325°F (160°C).
2. In a bowl, mix almond flour, melted butter, and 1/4 cup erythritol to make the crust.
3. Press the crust mixture into the bottom of a springform pan.
4. In a large bowl, beat cream cheese and 1/2 cup erythritol until smooth.
5. Add eggs one at a time, beating well after each addition.

6. Mix in vanilla extract and sour cream until well combined.
7. Pour the filling over the crust and smooth the top.
8. Bake for 50-60 minutes, or until the center is set.
9. Allow to cool, then refrigerate for at least 4 hours before serving.

85. Dark Chocolate Avocado Mousse

A rich and creamy dessert that's full of healthy fats and antioxidants.

Servings: 4
Preparation Time: 10 minutes
Cooking Time: None
Ingredients:

- 2 ripe avocados
- 1/4 cup (25 g) cocoa powder
- 1/4 cup (60 ml) almond milk
- 1/4 cup (60 ml) maple syrup or sweetener of choice
- 1 teaspoon (5 ml) vanilla extract
- A pinch of salt

Instructions:

1. In a food processor, combine avocados, cocoa powder, almond milk, maple syrup, vanilla extract, and salt.
2. Blend until smooth and creamy.
3. Divide into serving dishes and chill for at least 30 minutes before serving.

86. Pumpkin Spice Muffins

Deliciously spiced muffins that are perfect for fall or any time of year.

Servings: 12
Preparation Time: 15 minutes
Cooking Time: 25 minutes
Ingredients:

- 1 cup (120 g) almond flour
- 1/2 cup (60 g) coconut flour
- 1/2 cup (100 g) pumpkin puree
- 1/4 cup (60 ml) coconut oil, melted

- 1/4 cup (50 g) coconut sugar or sugar substitute
- 3 large eggs
- 1 teaspoon (5 ml) vanilla extract
- 1 teaspoon (5 g) baking powder
- 1 teaspoon (5 g) pumpkin pie spice
- A pinch of salt

Instructions:
1. Preheat oven to 350°F (175°C) and line a muffin tin with paper liners.
2. In a bowl, mix almond flour, coconut flour, coconut sugar, baking powder, pumpkin pie spice, and salt.
3. In another bowl, whisk together pumpkin puree, melted coconut oil, eggs, and vanilla extract.
4. Combine wet and dry ingredients, stirring until well mixed.
5. Divide the batter among the muffin cups.
6. Bake for 20-25 minutes, or until a toothpick inserted into the center comes out clean.
7. Let cool before serving.

87. Apple Cinnamon Crisp

A warm and comforting dessert that's full of natural sweetness.

Servings: 4
Preparation Time: 10 minutes
Cooking Time: 30 minutes
Ingredients:
- 4 apples, peeled, cored, and sliced
- 1/4 cup (60 ml) lemon juice
- 1/2 cup (50 g) almond flour
- 1/4 cup (30 g) rolled oats
- 1/4 cup (50 g) coconut sugar or sugar substitute
- 1 teaspoon (5 g) cinnamon
- 1/4 cup (60 ml) melted butter

Instructions:
1. Preheat oven to 350°F (175°C).
2. In a baking dish, toss apple slices with lemon juice.
3. In a bowl, mix almond flour, rolled oats, coconut sugar, cinnamon, and melted butter.
4. Sprinkle the mixture over the apples.
5. Bake for 25-30 minutes, or until apples are tender and the topping is golden brown.
6. Serve warm.

88. Peanut Butter Bliss Balls

A quick and satisfying treat that's perfect for a sweet snack.

Servings: 12 balls
Preparation Time: 10 minutes
Cooking Time: None
Ingredients:
- 1 cup (240 g) peanut butter
- 1/2 cup (45 g) rolled oats
- 1/4 cup (60 ml) honey or maple syrup
- 1/4 cup (30 g) flaxseed meal
- 1/4 cup (30 g) chocolate chips (optional)

Instructions:
1. In a bowl, mix peanut butter, rolled oats, honey, flaxseed meal, and chocolate chips.
2. Roll the mixture into 1-inch balls.
3. Refrigerate for at least 30 minutes before serving.
4. Store in an airtight container in the refrigerator.

89. Lemon Blueberry Bars

Bright and tangy, these bars are a delightful treat that's low in sugar and high in flavor.

Servings: 12
Preparation Time: 15 minutes
Cooking Time: 25 minutes
Ingredients:
- 1 cup (100 g) almond flour
- 1/2 cup (60 g) coconut flour
- 1/4 cup (60 ml) coconut oil, melted

- 1/4 cup (50 g) erythritol or sugar substitute
- 2 large eggs
- 1/2 cup (120 ml) fresh lemon juice
- 1 tablespoon (15 g) lemon zest
- 1 cup (150 g) fresh blueberries

Instructions:
1. Preheat the oven to 350°F (175°C) and line a baking dish with parchment paper.
2. In a bowl, mix almond flour, coconut flour, melted coconut oil, and half the erythritol until a dough forms.
3. Press the dough into the bottom of the baking dish and bake for 10 minutes.
4. In another bowl, whisk together eggs, lemon juice, lemon zest, and remaining erythritol.
5. Pour the lemon mixture over the baked crust and sprinkle blueberries on top.
6. Bake for another 15 minutes or until set.
7. Let cool before slicing into bars and serving.

90. Chocolate Chia Pudding
A creamy and rich pudding that's perfect for a healthy dessert or snack.
Servings: 4
Preparation Time: 10 minutes
Cooking Time: None (Refrigeration: 4 hours)
Ingredients:
- 1/4 cup (40 g) chia seeds
- 1 cup (240 ml) unsweetened almond milk
- 1/4 cup (25 g) cocoa powder
- 1/4 cup (60 ml) maple syrup or sweetener of choice
- 1 teaspoon (5 ml) vanilla extract

Instructions:
1. In a bowl, mix chia seeds, almond milk, cocoa powder, maple syrup, and vanilla extract.
2. Stir well and let sit for 5 minutes. Stir again to prevent clumping.

3. Cover and refrigerate for at least 4 hours or overnight.
4. Stir before serving and enjoy.

91. Carrot Cake Bites
Delicious bite-sized treats that taste just like carrot cake but are much healthier.
Servings: 12
Preparation Time: 15 minutes
Cooking Time: None
Ingredients:
- 1 cup (100 g) grated carrots
- 1/2 cup (60 g) almond flour
- 1/4 cup (60 ml) almond butter
- 1/4 cup (50 g) shredded coconut
- 1/4 cup (60 ml) maple syrup or honey
- 1 teaspoon (5 g) cinnamon
- 1/2 teaspoon (2.5 g) nutmeg
- 1/2 teaspoon (2.5 g) ginger

Instructions:
1. In a bowl, combine all ingredients and mix well.
2. Roll the mixture into 1-inch balls.
3. Refrigerate for at least 30 minutes before serving.
4. Store in an airtight container in the refrigerator.

92. Vanilla Bean Panna Cotta
A creamy and elegant dessert that's surprisingly easy to make.
Servings: 4
Preparation Time: 15 minutes
Cooking Time: 5 minutes (plus chilling time)
Ingredients:
- 1 cup (240 ml) unsweetened almond milk
- 1 cup (240 ml) heavy cream
- 1/4 cup (50 g) erythritol or sugar substitute
- 1 vanilla bean, split and seeds scraped
- 1 packet (7 g) unflavored gelatin

Instructions:

1. In a saucepan, heat almond milk, heavy cream, erythritol, vanilla bean seeds, and the pod over medium heat until simmering.
2. Remove from heat and discard the vanilla pod.
3. Sprinkle gelatin over the mixture and whisk until dissolved.
4. Pour into ramekins and refrigerate for at least 4 hours until set.
5. Serve chilled.

93. Mango Sorbet

A refreshing and naturally sweet dessert that's perfect for warm days.

Servings: 4
Preparation Time: 10 minutes
Cooking Time: None (Freezing: 2 hours)
Ingredients:

- 2 cups (300 g) diced mango
- 1/4 cup (60 ml) water
- 1 tablespoon (15 ml) lime juice

Instructions:

1. Blend diced mango, water, and lime juice until smooth.
2. Pour the mixture into a freezer-safe container.
3. Freeze for at least 2 hours, stirring every 30 minutes to prevent ice crystals.
4. Scoop and serve.

94. Raspberry Almond Tart

A delicious and visually appealing tart that's low in carbs and high in flavor.

Servings: 8
Preparation Time: 20 minutes
Cooking Time: 25 minutes
Ingredients:

- 1 cup (100 g) almond flour
- 1/4 cup (60 ml) coconut oil, melted
- 1/4 cup (50 g) erythritol or sugar substitute

- 1 cup (150 g) fresh raspberries
- 1/4 cup (30 g) sliced almonds
- 1 tablespoon (15 ml) honey (optional)

Instructions:

1. Preheat oven to 350°F (175°C) and grease a tart pan.
2. In a bowl, mix almond flour, melted coconut oil, and half the erythritol until a dough forms.
3. Press the dough into the bottom of the tart pan and bake for 10 minutes.
4. Arrange raspberries over the crust and sprinkle with sliced almonds.
5. Drizzle with honey if desired.
6. Bake for another 15 minutes until the almonds are golden brown.
7. Let cool before slicing and serving.

95. Zucchini Bread

A moist and flavorful bread that's perfect for a healthy dessert or snack.

Servings: 12
Preparation Time: 15 minutes
Cooking Time: 45 minutes
Ingredients:

- 1 cup (120 g) almond flour
- 1/2 cup (60 g) coconut flour
- 1 cup (150 g) grated zucchini
- 1/4 cup (60 ml) coconut oil, melted
- 1/4 cup (50 g) coconut sugar or sugar substitute
- 3 large eggs
- 1 teaspoon (5 ml) vanilla extract
- 1 teaspoon (5 g) baking powder
- 1 teaspoon (5 g) cinnamon
- A pinch of salt

Instructions:

1. Preheat oven to 350°F (175°C) and line a loaf pan with parchment paper.
2. In a bowl, mix almond flour, coconut flour, coconut sugar, baking powder, cinnamon, and salt.

3. In another bowl, whisk together grated zucchini, melted coconut oil, eggs, and vanilla extract.
4. Combine wet and dry ingredients, stirring until well mixed.
5. Pour the batter into the loaf pan.
6. Bake for 40-45 minutes, or until a toothpick inserted into the center comes out clean.
7. Let cool before slicing and serving.

96. Keto Chocolate Cake

A rich and decadent chocolate cake that's low in carbs and sugar-free.

Servings: 12
Preparation Time: 15 minutes
Cooking Time: 25 minutes
Ingredients:

- 1 cup (100 g) almond flour
- 1/2 cup (50 g) cocoa powder
- 1/2 cup (100 g) erythritol or sugar substitute
- 1/4 cup (60 ml) melted butter
- 4 large eggs
- 1 teaspoon (5 ml) vanilla extract
- 1 teaspoon (5 g) baking powder
- A pinch of salt

Instructions:

1. Preheat oven to 350°F (175°C) and grease a cake pan.
2. In a bowl, mix almond flour, cocoa powder, erythritol, baking powder, and salt.
3. In another bowl, whisk together melted butter, eggs, and vanilla extract.
4. Combine wet and dry ingredients, stirring until smooth.
5. Pour the batter into the cake pan and spread evenly.
6. Bake for 20-25 minutes, or until a toothpick inserted into the center comes out clean.
7. Let cool before frosting or serving.

97. Banana Nut Bread

A moist and flavorful bread that's perfect for a healthy dessert or snack.

Servings: 12
Preparation Time: 15 minutes
Cooking Time: 50 minutes
Ingredients:

- 2 ripe bananas, mashed
- 1/4 cup (60 ml) melted coconut oil
- 1/4 cup (50 g) erythritol or sugar substitute
- 2 large eggs
- 1 teaspoon (5 ml) vanilla extract
- 1 cup (100 g) almond flour
- 1/2 cup (60 g) coconut flour
- 1 teaspoon (5 g) baking soda
- 1/2 teaspoon (2.5 g) cinnamon
- 1/4 cup (30 g) chopped walnuts
- A pinch of salt

Instructions:

1. Preheat oven to 350°F (175°C) and grease a loaf pan.
2. In a large bowl, mix mashed bananas, melted coconut oil, erythritol, eggs, and vanilla extract.
3. In another bowl, combine almond flour, coconut flour, baking soda, cinnamon, and salt.
4. Add the dry ingredients to the wet ingredients and mix until well combined.
5. Fold in the chopped walnuts.
6. Pour the batter into the loaf pan and bake for 45-50 minutes, or until a toothpick inserted into the center comes out clean.
7. Let cool before slicing and serving.

98. Strawberry Shortcake

A light and refreshing dessert that's perfect for any occasion.

Servings: 8
Preparation Time: 20 minutes
Cooking Time: 15 minutes

Ingredients:

- 1 cup (100 g) almond flour
- 1/4 cup (60 ml) coconut oil, melted
- 1/4 cup (50 g) erythritol or sugar substitute
- 1 large egg
- 1 teaspoon (5 ml) vanilla extract
- 1/2 teaspoon (2.5 g) baking powder
- A pinch of salt
- 2 cups (300 g) fresh strawberries, sliced
- 1 cup (240 ml) whipped cream or coconut cream

Instructions:

1. Preheat oven to 350°F (175°C) and line a baking sheet with parchment paper.
2. In a bowl, mix almond flour, erythritol, baking powder, and salt.
3. In another bowl, whisk together melted coconut oil, egg, and vanilla extract.
4. Combine the wet and dry ingredients, stirring until a dough forms.
5. Scoop dough onto the baking sheet, flattening slightly to form shortcakes.
6. Bake for 12-15 minutes, or until golden brown.
7. Let cool before assembling the shortcakes.
8. To assemble, layer sliced strawberries and whipped cream between the shortcakes.
9. Serve immediately.

99. Lemon Yogurt Cake

A tangy and moist cake that's perfect for a light dessert.

Servings: 10
Preparation Time: 15 minutes
Cooking Time: 35 minutes
Ingredients:

- 1 cup (120 g) almond flour
- 1/2 cup (60 g) coconut flour
- 1/2 cup (120 ml) Greek yogurt
- 1/4 cup (60 ml) coconut oil, melted

- 1/4 cup (50 g) erythritol or sugar substitute
- 3 large eggs
- 1 teaspoon (5 ml) vanilla extract
- 1 teaspoon (5 g) baking powder
- 1/4 cup (60 ml) fresh lemon juice
- 1 tablespoon (15 g) lemon zest
- A pinch of salt

Instructions:

1. Preheat oven to 350°F (175°C) and grease a cake pan.
2. In a bowl, mix almond flour, coconut flour, erythritol, baking powder, lemon zest, and salt.
3. In another bowl, whisk together Greek yogurt, melted coconut oil, eggs, vanilla extract, and lemon juice.
4. Combine the wet and dry ingredients, stirring until well mixed.
5. Pour the batter into the cake pan and bake for 30-35 minutes, or until a toothpick inserted into the center comes out clean.
6. Let cool before slicing and serving.

100. Coconut Macaroons

Chewy and delicious macaroons that are naturally sweet and satisfying.

Servings: 12
Preparation Time: 10 minutes
Cooking Time: 20 minutes
Ingredients:

- 2 cups (200 g) shredded coconut
- 1/4 cup (60 ml) coconut milk
- 1/4 cup (50 g) erythritol or sugar substitute
- 2 large egg whites
- 1 teaspoon (5 ml) vanilla extract
- A pinch of salt

Instructions:

1. Preheat oven to 325°F (160°C) and line a baking sheet with parchment paper.

2. In a bowl, mix shredded coconut, coconut milk, erythritol, vanilla extract, and salt.
3. In another bowl, beat egg whites until stiff peaks form.
4. Gently fold the beaten egg whites into the coconut mixture.
5. Scoop the mixture onto the baking sheet, forming small mounds.
6. Bake for 20 minutes, or until the edges are golden brown.
7. Let cool before serving.

Chapter 11: Appetizing Appetizers

Appetizers are a great way to start a meal, offering a taste of what's to come while whetting your appetite. For those managing diabetes, it's important to choose appetizers that are not only delicious but also supportive of your health goals. This chapter features a variety of appetizing, diabetes-friendly starters that are perfect for any occasion.

101. Stuffed Mushrooms

These savory stuffed mushrooms are a delightful bite-sized treat, perfect for any gathering.

Servings: 4
Preparation Time: 15 minutes
Cooking Time: 20 minutes
Ingredients:

- 12 large mushrooms, stems removed
- 1/4 cup (30 g) breadcrumbs
- 1/4 cup (30 g) grated Parmesan cheese
- 2 tablespoons (30 ml) olive oil
- 2 garlic cloves, minced
- 1/4 cup (30 g) chopped fresh parsley
- Salt and pepper to taste

Instructions:

1. Preheat oven to 375°F (190°C).
2. In a bowl, mix breadcrumbs, Parmesan cheese, olive oil, garlic, parsley, salt, and pepper.
3. Stuff each mushroom cap with the breadcrumb mixture.
4. Place mushrooms on a baking sheet and bake for 20 minutes until golden brown.
5. Serve warm.

102. Caprese Skewers

A fresh and simple appetizer that combines classic Caprese flavors into a convenient skewer.

Servings: 4
Preparation Time: 10 minutes
Cooking Time: None
Ingredients:

- 12 cherry tomatoes
- 12 small mozzarella balls
- Fresh basil leaves
- 1 tablespoon (15 ml) balsamic glaze
- 1 tablespoon (15 ml) olive oil
- Salt and pepper to taste
- Skewers

Instructions:

1. Thread a cherry tomato, mozzarella ball, and basil leaf onto each skewer.
2. Arrange on a serving platter.
3. Drizzle with balsamic glaze and olive oil.
4. Season with salt and pepper.
5. Serve immediately.

103. Guacamole Deviled Eggs

A creamy and flavorful twist on traditional deviled eggs, perfect for a low-carb snack.

Servings: 4
Preparation Time: 15 minutes
Cooking Time: 10 minutes
Ingredients:

- 6 hard-boiled eggs, peeled
- 1 ripe avocado
- 1 tablespoon (15 ml) lime juice
- 1 tablespoon (15 ml) chopped cilantro
- Salt and pepper to taste
- Paprika for garnish

Instructions:

1. Cut the eggs in half and remove the yolks.
2. In a bowl, mash the avocado and mix with egg yolks, lime juice, cilantro, salt, and pepper.
3. Spoon the mixture back into the egg whites.
4. Sprinkle with paprika.
5. Serve immediately.

104. Cucumber Bites

A refreshing and light appetizer that's quick to make and delightful to eat.

Servings: 4
Preparation Time: 10 minutes
Cooking Time: None
Ingredients:

- 1 cucumber, sliced into rounds
- 1/4 cup (60 g) cream cheese, softened
- 1 tablespoon (15 g) fresh dill, chopped
- Salt and pepper to taste

Instructions:

1. Spread a small amount of cream cheese on each cucumber slice.
2. Sprinkle with fresh dill.
3. Season with salt and pepper.
4. Serve immediately.

105. Mini Quiches

These mini quiches are packed with flavor and perfect for any occasion.

Servings: 12
Preparation Time: 15 minutes
Cooking Time: 20 minutes
Ingredients:

- 4 large eggs
- 1/2 cup (120 ml) milk
- 1/2 cup (50 g) shredded cheese
- 1/4 cup (30 g) diced ham or cooked bacon
- 1/4 cup (30 g) chopped spinach
- Salt and pepper to taste

Instructions:

1. Preheat oven to 375°F (190°C) and grease a muffin tin.
2. In a bowl, whisk together eggs, milk, salt, and pepper.
3. Divide ham and spinach among the muffin cups.
4. Pour the egg mixture over the fillings.
5. Sprinkle with cheese.
6. Bake for 15-20 minutes until set.
7. Serve warm.

106. Shrimp Cocktail

A classic appetizer that's both elegant and easy to prepare.

Servings: 4
Preparation Time: 10 minutes
Cooking Time: 5 minutes
Ingredients:

- 1 pound (450 g) large shrimp, peeled and deveined
- 1 lemon, halved
- 1/2 cup (120 ml) cocktail sauce
- Fresh parsley for garnish

Instructions:

1. Bring a large pot of water to a boil and squeeze in the juice of half the lemon.
2. Add the shrimp and cook for 2-3 minutes until pink and opaque.
3. Drain and cool under cold running water.
4. Arrange shrimp on a platter with cocktail sauce and lemon wedges.
5. Garnish with fresh parsley.
6. Serve chilled.

107. Spicy Chicken Wings

These wings are baked to perfection and coated in a deliciously spicy sauce.

Servings: 4
Preparation Time: 10 minutes
Cooking Time: 40 minutes
Ingredients:

- 1 pound (450 g) chicken wings
- 2 tablespoons (30 ml) olive oil
- 1/4 cup (60 ml) hot sauce
- 1 tablespoon (15 g) butter, melted
- 1 teaspoon (5 g) garlic powder
- Salt and pepper to taste

Instructions:

1. Preheat oven to 400°F (200°C).
2. Toss chicken wings with olive oil, garlic powder, salt, and pepper.
3. Arrange wings on a baking sheet and bake for 35-40 minutes until crispy.

4. In a bowl, mix hot sauce and melted butter.
5. Toss the baked wings in the sauce.
6. Serve immediately.

108. Veggie Spring Rolls

Fresh and colorful, these spring rolls are a healthy and tasty appetizer.

Servings: 4
Preparation Time: 20 minutes
Cooking Time: None
Ingredients:

- 8 rice paper wrappers
- 1 cup (150 g) shredded carrots
- 1 cup (150 g) shredded cabbage
- 1 cup (150 g) cooked shrimp, sliced (optional)
- 1/2 cup (75 g) fresh basil leaves
- 1/2 cup (75 g) fresh mint leaves
- 1/2 cup (75 g) fresh cilantro leaves
- 1/4 cup (60 ml) hoisin sauce
- 1 tablespoon (15 ml) soy sauce

Instructions:

1. Dip a rice paper wrapper in warm water for a few seconds until soft.
2. Lay the wrapper on a flat surface and place a small amount of each filling ingredient in the center.
3. Fold the sides over the filling and roll up tightly.
4. Repeat with remaining wrappers and fillings.
5. Mix hoisin sauce and soy sauce for dipping.
6. Serve immediately.

109. Bruschetta with Tomato and Basil

A classic Italian appetizer that's fresh, flavorful, and easy to prepare.

Servings: 4
Preparation Time: 10 minutes
Cooking Time: 5 minutes
Ingredients:

- 4 slices whole grain baguette
- 2 large tomatoes, diced
- 1/4 cup (30 g) fresh basil, chopped
- 2 tablespoons (30 ml) olive oil
- 1 garlic clove, minced
- Salt and pepper to taste
- Balsamic glaze (optional)

Instructions:

1. Preheat oven to 400°F (200°C).
2. Arrange baguette slices on a baking sheet and brush with olive oil.
3. Toast in the oven for 5 minutes until golden brown.
4. In a bowl, mix diced tomatoes, basil, garlic, salt, and pepper.
5. Spoon the tomato mixture onto the toasted bread.
6. Drizzle with balsamic glaze if desired.
7. Serve immediately.

110. Smoked Salmon Roll-Ups

These elegant roll-ups are perfect for a sophisticated appetizer or a light snack.

Servings: 4
Preparation Time: 10 minutes
Cooking Time: None
Ingredients:

- 4 ounces (115 g) smoked salmon slices
- 1/4 cup (60 g) cream cheese, softened
- 1 tablespoon (15 g) fresh dill, chopped
- 1 teaspoon (5 ml) lemon juice
- 1 cucumber, sliced thinly

Instructions:

1. In a bowl, mix cream cheese, dill, and lemon juice.
2. Spread a thin layer of the cream cheese mixture onto each smoked salmon slice.
3. Place a cucumber slice on one end of the salmon and roll up tightly.
4. Secure with toothpicks if necessary.
5. Serve immediately.

111. Cheese Stuffed Peppers

Sweet mini bell peppers filled with a creamy cheese mixture for a delightful bite.

Servings: 4
Preparation Time: 10 minutes
Cooking Time: None
Ingredients:

- 12 mini bell peppers, halved and seeded
- 1/2 cup (120 g) cream cheese, softened
- 1/4 cup (30 g) shredded cheddar cheese
- 1 tablespoon (15 g) fresh chives, chopped
- Salt and pepper to taste

Instructions:

1. In a bowl, mix cream cheese, cheddar cheese, chives, salt, and pepper.
2. Spoon the cheese mixture into the bell pepper halves.
3. Arrange on a platter and serve immediately.

112. Meat and Cheese Platter

A simple yet elegant appetizer that's perfect for entertaining.

Servings: 4
Preparation Time: 10 minutes
Cooking Time: None
Ingredients:

- 4 ounces (115 g) assorted cured meats (salami, prosciutto, etc.)
- 4 ounces (115 g) assorted cheeses (cheddar, brie, etc.)
- 1/4 cup (60 g) mixed olives
- 1/4 cup (60 g) nuts (almonds, walnuts, etc.)
- Fresh grapes or apple slices for garnish

Instructions:

1. Arrange the cured meats, cheeses, olives, and nuts on a platter.
2. Garnish with fresh grapes or apple slices.
3. Serve immediately.

113. Eggplant Dip

A creamy and flavorful dip that's perfect with fresh vegetables or whole grain crackers.

Servings: 4
Preparation Time: 10 minutes
Cooking Time: 20 minutes
Ingredients:

- 1 large eggplant
- 2 tablespoons (30 ml) olive oil
- 1 garlic clove, minced
- 1 tablespoon (15 ml) lemon juice
- Salt and pepper to taste
- Fresh parsley for garnish

Instructions:

1. Preheat oven to 400°F (200°C).
2. Cut the eggplant in half, drizzle with olive oil, and roast for 20 minutes until tender.
3. Scoop out the eggplant flesh and place in a food processor.
4. Add garlic, lemon juice, salt, and pepper. Blend until smooth.
5. Transfer to a bowl, garnish with fresh parsley, and serve with veggies or crackers.

114. Cauliflower Bites

Bite-sized cauliflower pieces that are crispy on the outside and tender on the inside.

Servings: 4
Preparation Time: 10 minutes
Cooking Time: 25 minutes
Ingredients:

- 1 head cauliflower, cut into bite-sized pieces
- 2 tablespoons (30 ml) olive oil
- 1/4 cup (30 g) grated Parmesan cheese
- 1 teaspoon (5 g) garlic powder
- Salt and pepper to taste

Instructions:

1. Preheat oven to 425°F (220°C).

2. Toss cauliflower pieces with olive oil, Parmesan cheese, garlic powder, salt, and pepper.
3. Spread on a baking sheet and roast for 20-25 minutes until golden and crispy.
4. Serve immediately.

115. Prosciutto Wrapped Asparagus
A simple and elegant appetizer that's sure to impress your guests.
Servings: 4
Preparation Time: 10 minutes
Cooking Time: 15 minutes
Ingredients:
- 12 asparagus spears, trimmed
- 6 slices prosciutto, halved lengthwise
- 1 tablespoon (15 ml) olive oil
- Salt and pepper to taste

Instructions:
1. Preheat oven to 400°F (200°C).
2. Wrap each asparagus spear with a strip of prosciutto.
3. Place on a baking sheet and drizzle with olive oil.
4. Season with salt and pepper.
5. Bake for 12-15 minutes until asparagus is tender and prosciutto is crispy.
6. Serve immediately.

116. Spicy Tuna Tartare
A flavorful and sophisticated appetizer that's perfect for seafood lovers.
Servings: 4
Preparation Time: 15 minutes
Cooking Time: None
Ingredients:
- 1/2 pound (225 g) sushi-grade tuna, diced
- 1 tablespoon (15 ml) soy sauce
- 1 tablespoon (15 ml) sesame oil
- 1 teaspoon (5 ml) sriracha sauce
- 1 avocado, diced
- 1/4 cup (30 g) diced cucumber

- 1 tablespoon (15 g) sesame seeds
- Fresh cilantro for garnish

Instructions:
1. In a bowl, mix soy sauce, sesame oil, and sriracha sauce.
2. Add diced tuna, avocado, cucumber, and sesame seeds. Toss gently to combine.
3. Garnish with fresh cilantro.
4. Serve immediately with cucumber slices or whole grain crackers.

117. Veggie Platter with Hummus
A colorful and nutritious platter that's perfect for sharing.
Servings: 4
Preparation Time: 10 minutes
Cooking Time: None
Ingredients:
- 1 cup (240 g) hummus
- 1 carrot, cut into sticks
- 1 cucumber, cut into sticks
- 1 bell pepper, sliced
- 1 cup (150 g) cherry tomatoes
- 1 cup (150 g) snap peas

Instructions:
1. Arrange the vegetables on a large platter.
2. Place the hummus in a bowl in the center of the platter.
3. Serve immediately.

118. Zucchini Fritters
Crispy on the outside and tender on the inside, these fritters are a delightful snack.
Servings: 4
Preparation Time: 15 minutes
Cooking Time: 10 minutes
Ingredients:
- 2 large zucchinis, grated
- 1/4 cup (30 g) almond flour
- 1/4 cup (30 g) grated Parmesan cheese
- 1 large egg
- 1 garlic clove, minced
- Salt and pepper to taste

- 2 tablespoons (30 ml) olive oil

Instructions:

1. Place the grated zucchini in a clean towel and squeeze out excess moisture.
2. In a bowl, combine zucchini, almond flour, Parmesan cheese, egg, garlic, salt, and pepper.
3. Heat olive oil in a large skillet over medium heat.
4. Scoop small amounts of the mixture into the skillet and flatten into patties.
5. Cook for 3-4 minutes on each side until golden brown.
6. Serve warm.

119. Chicken Satay

Tender and flavorful chicken skewers served with a delicious peanut sauce.

Servings: 4
Preparation Time: 15 minutes
Cooking Time: 10 minutes
Ingredients:

- 1 pound (450 g) chicken breast, cut into strips
- 1/4 cup (60 ml) coconut milk
- 2 tablespoons (30 ml) soy sauce
- 1 tablespoon (15 ml) lime juice
- 1 tablespoon (15 ml) honey
- 1 teaspoon (5 g) curry powder
- Wooden skewers, soaked in water

Peanut Sauce:

- 1/4 cup (60 ml) peanut butter
- 2 tablespoons (30 ml) soy sauce
- 1 tablespoon (15 ml) lime juice
- 1 tablespoon (15 ml) honey
- 1 garlic clove, minced
- Water to thin, if needed

Instructions:

1. In a bowl, mix coconut milk, soy sauce, lime juice, honey, and curry powder. Add chicken strips and marinate for at least 30 minutes.
2. Thread chicken onto skewers.
3. Heat a grill or grill pan over medium-high heat and cook chicken skewers for 3-4 minutes on each side until fully cooked.
4. For the peanut sauce, mix all ingredients in a bowl, adding water to achieve desired consistency.
5. Serve chicken skewers with peanut sauce.

120. Greek Yogurt Dip

A creamy and tangy dip that's perfect with fresh veggies or whole grain crackers.

Servings: 4
Preparation Time: 10 minutes
Cooking Time: None
Ingredients:

- 1 cup (240 ml) Greek yogurt
- 1/4 cup (30 g) cucumber, finely chopped
- 1 garlic clove, minced
- 1 tablespoon (15 ml) lemon juice
- 1 tablespoon (15 g) fresh dill, chopped
- Salt and pepper to taste

Instructions:

1. In a bowl, combine Greek yogurt, cucumber, garlic, lemon juice, dill, salt, and pepper.
2. Mix well and refrigerate for at least 30 minutes to let the flavors meld.
3. Serve with fresh veggies or whole grain crackers.

Chapter 12: Fabulous Fish and Seafood

Fish and seafood are not only delicious but also packed with nutrients that are beneficial for managing diabetes. They are excellent sources of lean protein and healthy fats, particularly omega-3 fatty acids, which can help reduce inflammation and support heart health. This chapter offers a variety of fabulous fish and seafood recipes that are both flavorful and diabetes-friendly.

121. Grilled Salmon with Avocado Salsa

A fresh and zesty dish that combines perfectly grilled salmon with a creamy avocado salsa.

Servings: 2
Preparation Time: 10 minutes
Cooking Time: 10 minutes
Ingredients:

- 2 salmon fillets
- 1 tablespoon (15 ml) olive oil
- Salt and pepper to taste
- 1 avocado, diced
- 1 small tomato, diced
- 1/4 cup (30 g) red onion, finely chopped
- 1 tablespoon (15 ml) lime juice
- 1 tablespoon (15 g) fresh cilantro, chopped

Instructions:

1. Preheat grill to medium-high heat.
2. Brush salmon fillets with olive oil and season with salt and pepper.
3. Grill salmon for 4-5 minutes on each side, until fully cooked.
4. In a bowl, combine avocado, tomato, red onion, lime juice, and cilantro.
5. Serve the grilled salmon topped with avocado salsa.

122. Lemon Butter Shrimp

A simple yet flavorful dish that's quick to prepare and perfect for any meal.

Servings: 2
Preparation Time: 10 minutes
Cooking Time: 10 minutes
Ingredients:

- 1/2 pound (225 g) shrimp, peeled and deveined
- 2 tablespoons (30 g) butter
- 2 garlic cloves, minced
- Juice of 1 lemon
- 1 tablespoon (15 g) fresh parsley, chopped
- Salt and pepper to taste

Instructions:

1. Heat butter in a large skillet over medium heat.
2. Add garlic and sauté for 1 minute until fragrant.
3. Add shrimp and cook for 2-3 minutes on each side until pink and opaque.
4. Add lemon juice and parsley, season with salt and pepper.
5. Serve immediately.

123. Baked Tilapia with Herbs

A light and healthy dish that's packed with fresh herbs and flavor.

Servings: 2
Preparation Time: 10 minutes
Cooking Time: 15 minutes
Ingredients:

- 2 tilapia fillets
- 1 tablespoon (15 ml) olive oil
- 1 tablespoon (15 g) fresh dill, chopped
- 1 tablespoon (15 g) fresh parsley, chopped
- 1 teaspoon (5 g) garlic powder
- Salt and pepper to taste

Instructions:

1. Preheat oven to 375°F (190°C).
2. Place tilapia fillets on a baking sheet and brush with olive oil.

3. Sprinkle with dill, parsley, garlic powder, salt, and pepper.
4. Bake for 12-15 minutes until the fish flakes easily with a fork.
5. Serve hot.

124. Seared Scallops with Garlic Butter

Elegant and delicious, these scallops are perfect for a special dinner.

Servings: 2
Preparation Time: 10 minutes
Cooking Time: 5 minutes
Ingredients:

- 1/2 pound (225 g) large scallops
- 2 tablespoons (30 g) butter
- 2 garlic cloves, minced
- 1 tablespoon (15 g) fresh parsley, chopped
- Salt and pepper to taste

Instructions:

1. Pat scallops dry and season with salt and pepper.
2. Heat butter in a large skillet over medium-high heat.
3. Add garlic and sauté for 1 minute until fragrant.
4. Add scallops and sear for 2-3 minutes on each side until golden brown.
5. Sprinkle with parsley and serve immediately.

125. Fish Tacos with Slaw

A fun and healthy dish that's perfect for a casual meal.

Servings: 4
Preparation Time: 15 minutes
Cooking Time: 10 minutes
Ingredients:

- 1 pound (450 g) white fish fillets (such as cod or tilapia)
- 1 tablespoon (15 ml) olive oil
- 1 teaspoon (5 g) chili powder
- 1 teaspoon (5 g) cumin
- 1/2 teaspoon (2.5 g) garlic powder
- Salt and pepper to taste
- 8 small whole grain tortillas
- 2 cups (150 g) shredded cabbage
- 1/4 cup (60 ml) Greek yogurt
- 1 tablespoon (15 ml) lime juice
- Fresh cilantro for garnish

Instructions:

1. Preheat grill or skillet over medium-high heat.
2. Brush fish with olive oil and season with chili powder, cumin, garlic powder, salt, and pepper.
3. Grill or cook fish for 3-4 minutes on each side until fully cooked.
4. In a bowl, mix shredded cabbage, Greek yogurt, and lime juice.
5. Warm tortillas and fill with fish and slaw.
6. Garnish with fresh cilantro and serve immediately.

126. Shrimp and Veggie Skewers

Colorful and tasty skewers that are perfect for grilling season.

Servings: 4
Preparation Time: 15 minutes
Cooking Time: 10 minutes
Ingredients:

- 1 pound (450 g) shrimp, peeled and deveined
- 1 red bell pepper, cut into chunks
- 1 yellow bell pepper, cut into chunks
- 1 zucchini, sliced
- 1 red onion, cut into chunks
- 2 tablespoons (30 ml) olive oil
- 1 tablespoon (15 ml) lemon juice
- Salt and pepper to taste
- Wooden or metal skewers

Instructions:

1. Preheat grill to medium-high heat.
2. In a bowl, mix olive oil, lemon juice, salt, and pepper.

3. Thread shrimp and vegetables onto skewers.
4. Brush with olive oil mixture.
5. Grill for 2-3 minutes on each side until shrimp are pink and vegetables are tender.
6. Serve immediately.

127. Tuna Steaks with Mango Salsa

A refreshing and flavorful dish that's perfect for a summer meal.

Servings: 2
Preparation Time: 15 minutes
Cooking Time: 10 minutes
Ingredients:
- 2 tuna steaks
- 1 tablespoon (15 ml) olive oil
- Salt and pepper to taste
- 1 mango, diced
- 1/4 cup (30 g) red onion, finely chopped
- 1 jalapeño, seeded and finely chopped
- 1 tablespoon (15 ml) lime juice
- 1 tablespoon (15 g) fresh cilantro, chopped

Instructions:
1. Preheat grill to medium-high heat.
2. Brush tuna steaks with olive oil and season with salt and pepper.
3. Grill tuna for 3-4 minutes on each side until seared but still pink in the center.
4. In a bowl, combine mango, red onion, jalapeño, lime juice, and cilantro.
5. Serve tuna steaks topped with mango salsa.

128. Baked Cod with Lemon

A light and flavorful dish that's easy to prepare and perfect for a healthy dinner.

Servings: 2
Preparation Time: 10 minutes
Cooking Time: 15 minutes
Ingredients:
- 2 cod fillets
- 2 tablespoons (30 ml) olive oil
- 1 lemon, sliced
- 1 teaspoon (5 g) garlic powder
- Salt and pepper to taste
- Fresh parsley for garnish

Instructions:
1. Preheat oven to 400°F (200°C).
2. Place cod fillets on a baking sheet and drizzle with olive oil.
3. Season with garlic powder, salt, and pepper.
4. Arrange lemon slices on top of the fillets.
5. Bake for 12-15 minutes until the fish flakes easily with a fork.
6. Garnish with fresh parsley and serve immediately.

129. Crab Cakes

These crab cakes are light, flavorful, and perfect for a satisfying meal or appetizer.

Servings: 4
Preparation Time: 15 minutes
Cooking Time: 10 minutes
Ingredients:
- 1 pound (450 g) lump crab meat
- 1/4 cup (30 g) breadcrumbs
- 1/4 cup (30 g) finely chopped red bell pepper
- 1/4 cup (30 g) finely chopped green onion
- 1 egg, beaten
- 2 tablespoons (30 ml) mayonnaise
- 1 tablespoon (15 ml) Dijon mustard
- 1 tablespoon (15 ml) lemon juice
- 1 teaspoon (5 ml) Worcestershire sauce
- Salt and pepper to taste
- 2 tablespoons (30 ml) olive oil

Instructions:
1. In a large bowl, combine crab meat, breadcrumbs, bell pepper, green onion, egg, mayonnaise, Dijon mustard, lemon juice, Worcestershire sauce, salt, and pepper.

2. Form the mixture into patties.
3. Heat olive oil in a large skillet over medium heat.
4. Cook the crab cakes for 4-5 minutes on each side until golden brown.
5. Serve immediately.

130. Grilled Mahi-Mahi

A simple and flavorful dish that's perfect for a healthy dinner.

Servings: 2
Preparation Time: 10 minutes
Cooking Time: 10 minutes
Ingredients:

- 2 mahi-mahi fillets
- 2 tablespoons (30 ml) olive oil
- 1 tablespoon (15 ml) lime juice
- 1 teaspoon (5 g) garlic powder
- 1 teaspoon (5 g) paprika
- Salt and pepper to taste

Instructions:

1. Preheat grill to medium-high heat.
2. Brush mahi-mahi fillets with olive oil and lime juice.
3. Season with garlic powder, paprika, salt, and pepper.
4. Grill the fillets for 4-5 minutes on each side until fully cooked.
5. Serve immediately.

131. Salmon Patties

These salmon patties are crispy on the outside and tender on the inside.

Servings: 4
Preparation Time: 15 minutes
Cooking Time: 10 minutes
Ingredients:

- 1 can (14.75 ounces) salmon, drained and flaked
- 1/4 cup (30 g) breadcrumbs
- 1/4 cup (30 g) finely chopped onion
- 1 egg, beaten
- 2 tablespoons (30 ml) mayonnaise

- 1 tablespoon (15 ml) lemon juice
- 1 teaspoon (5 g) Dijon mustard
- Salt and pepper to taste
- 2 tablespoons (30 ml) olive oil

Instructions:

1. In a large bowl, combine salmon, breadcrumbs, onion, egg, mayonnaise, lemon juice, Dijon mustard, salt, and pepper.
2. Form the mixture into patties.
3. Heat olive oil in a large skillet over medium heat.
4. Cook the patties for 4-5 minutes on each side until golden brown.
5. Serve immediately.

132. Lobster Tail with Garlic Butter

A luxurious and indulgent dish that's perfect for a special occasion.

Servings: 2
Preparation Time: 10 minutes
Cooking Time: 15 minutes
Ingredients:

- 2 lobster tails
- 1/4 cup (60 g) butter
- 2 garlic cloves, minced
- 1 tablespoon (15 ml) lemon juice
- 1 tablespoon (15 g) fresh parsley, chopped
- Salt and pepper to taste

Instructions:

1. Preheat oven to 425°F (220°C).
2. Using kitchen shears, cut the top shell of each lobster tail lengthwise.
3. Pull the shell apart slightly and lift the meat, laying it on top of the shell.
4. In a small saucepan, melt butter and add garlic, lemon juice, parsley, salt, and pepper.
5. Brush the lobster tails with the garlic butter mixture.

6. Place the lobster tails on a baking sheet and bake for 12-15 minutes until the meat is opaque and cooked through.
7. Serve immediately.

133. Ceviche

A fresh and tangy seafood dish that's perfect for a light meal or appetizer.

Servings: 4
Preparation Time: 15 minutes
Cooking Time: None (Chill time: 30 minutes)
Ingredients:

- 1 pound (450 g) firm white fish (such as halibut or tilapia), diced
- 1/2 cup (120 ml) lime juice
- 1/2 cup (75 g) diced red onion
- 1 tomato, diced
- 1 jalapeño, seeded and finely chopped
- 1/4 cup (30 g) chopped fresh cilantro
- Salt and pepper to taste

Instructions:

1. In a large bowl, combine fish and lime juice. Make sure the fish is fully submerged.
2. Cover and refrigerate for 30 minutes until the fish is opaque and "cooked" by the lime juice.
3. Drain the lime juice from the fish.
4. Add red onion, tomato, jalapeño, cilantro, salt, and pepper.
5. Toss gently to combine and serve immediately.

134. Pan-Seared Trout

A simple yet elegant dish that highlights the delicate flavor of trout.

Servings: 2
Preparation Time: 10 minutes
Cooking Time: 10 minutes
Ingredients:

- 2 trout fillets
- 2 tablespoons (30 ml) olive oil
- Salt and pepper to taste

- 1 lemon, sliced
- Fresh parsley for garnish

Instructions:

1. Heat olive oil in a large skillet over medium-high heat.
2. Season trout fillets with salt and pepper.
3. Place the fillets skin-side down in the skillet and cook for 3-4 minutes.
4. Flip the fillets and cook for an additional 2-3 minutes until the fish is cooked through.
5. Serve with lemon slices and garnish with fresh parsley.

135. Baked Halibut

A light and flaky fish that's perfect for a healthy and satisfying meal.

Servings: 2
Preparation Time: 10 minutes
Cooking Time: 20 minutes
Ingredients:

- 2 halibut fillets
- 2 tablespoons (30 ml) olive oil
- 1 teaspoon (5 g) garlic powder
- 1 teaspoon (5 g) paprika
- Salt and pepper to taste
- Fresh dill for garnish

Instructions:

1. Preheat oven to 400°F (200°C).
2. Place halibut fillets on a baking sheet and brush with olive oil.
3. Season with garlic powder, paprika, salt, and pepper.
4. Bake for 18-20 minutes until the fish flakes easily with a fork.
5. Garnish with fresh dill and serve immediately.

136. Shrimp Scampi

A classic and flavorful dish that's perfect for a quick and delicious dinner.

Servings: 4
Preparation Time: 10 minutes
Cooking Time: 10 minutes
Ingredients:

- 1 pound (450 g) shrimp, peeled and deveined
- 3 tablespoons (45 g) butter
- 4 garlic cloves, minced
- 1/4 cup (60 ml) white wine
- 1/4 cup (60 ml) chicken broth
- 2 tablespoons (30 ml) lemon juice
- 1/4 cup (30 g) chopped fresh parsley
- Salt and pepper to taste

Instructions:

1. Heat butter in a large skillet over medium heat.
2. Add garlic and sauté for 1 minute until fragrant.
3. Add shrimp and cook for 2-3 minutes on each side until pink and opaque.
4. Stir in white wine, chicken broth, and lemon juice.
5. Cook for an additional 2 minutes until the sauce is slightly reduced.
6. Stir in fresh parsley and season with salt and pepper.
7. Serve immediately.

137. Mussels in White Wine Sauce

A classic and elegant dish that's both simple to prepare and full of flavor.

Servings: 4
Preparation Time: 10 minutes
Cooking Time: 10 minutes
Ingredients:

- 2 pounds (900 g) mussels, cleaned and debearded
- 1 cup (240 ml) dry white wine
- 2 tablespoons (30 ml) olive oil
- 2 garlic cloves, minced
- 1 shallot, finely chopped
- 1/4 cup (30 g) fresh parsley, chopped
- Salt and pepper to taste
- Lemon wedges for serving

Instructions:

1. Heat olive oil in a large pot over medium heat.
2. Add garlic and shallot, sauté until fragrant.
3. Pour in the white wine and bring to a simmer.
4. Add the mussels, cover, and cook for 5-7 minutes until the mussels open.
5. Discard any mussels that do not open.
6. Stir in fresh parsley, season with salt and pepper.
7. Serve immediately with lemon wedges.

138. Fish and Veggie Foil Packs

An easy and healthy meal that's perfect for grilling or baking.

Servings: 4
Preparation Time: 10 minutes
Cooking Time: 20 minutes
Ingredients:

- 4 white fish fillets (such as cod or tilapia)
- 1 zucchini, sliced
- 1 yellow squash, sliced
- 1 red bell pepper, sliced
- 1 lemon, sliced
- 4 tablespoons (60 ml) olive oil
- 1 teaspoon (5 g) garlic powder
- Salt and pepper to taste

Instructions:

1. Preheat grill to medium-high heat or oven to 400°F (200°C).
2. Cut four large pieces of aluminum foil.
3. Place one fish fillet and a portion of vegetables on each piece of foil.
4. Drizzle with olive oil and season with garlic powder, salt, and pepper.
5. Top with lemon slices.

6. Fold the foil into packets, sealing the edges tightly.
7. Grill or bake for 20 minutes until the fish is cooked through and vegetables are tender.
8. Serve hot.

139. Sautéed Clams

A quick and flavorful dish that's perfect for a light meal or appetizer.

Servings: 4
Preparation Time: 10 minutes
Cooking Time: 10 minutes
Ingredients:

- 2 pounds (900 g) clams, cleaned
- 2 tablespoons (30 ml) olive oil
- 2 garlic cloves, minced
- 1/2 cup (120 ml) dry white wine
- 1/4 cup (30 g) fresh parsley, chopped
- Salt and pepper to taste
- Lemon wedges for serving

Instructions:

1. Heat olive oil in a large skillet over medium heat.
2. Add garlic and sauté until fragrant.
3. Pour in the white wine and bring to a simmer.
4. Add the clams, cover, and cook for 5-7 minutes until the clams open.
5. Discard any clams that do not open.
6. Stir in fresh parsley, season with salt and pepper.
7. Serve immediately with lemon wedges.

140. Garlic Parmesan Crusted Salmon

A delicious and easy-to-make dish that's perfect for any occasion.

Servings: 4
Preparation Time: 10 minutes
Cooking Time: 15 minutes
Ingredients:

- 4 salmon fillets
- 1/4 cup (30 g) grated Parmesan cheese
- 1/4 cup (30 g) breadcrumbs
- 2 garlic cloves, minced
- 2 tablespoons (30 ml) olive oil
- Salt and pepper to taste
- Lemon wedges for serving

Instructions:

1. Preheat oven to 400°F (200°C).
2. In a bowl, mix Parmesan cheese, breadcrumbs, garlic, and olive oil.
3. Season salmon fillets with salt and pepper.
4. Press the Parmesan mixture onto the top of each fillet.
5. Place the fillets on a baking sheet and bake for 12-15 minutes until the salmon is cooked through and the crust is golden brown.
6. Serve immediately with lemon wedges.

Chapter 13: Vibrant Vegetarian

Incorporating more plant-based meals into your diet is a great way to boost your health, particularly for managing diabetes. Vegetarian dishes can be packed with nutrients, fiber, and flavor, making them a satisfying and wholesome choice. This chapter offers a variety of vibrant, diabetes-friendly vegetarian recipes that are both delicious and nutritious.

141. Stuffed Bell Peppers

A colorful and nutritious dish that's perfect for a hearty meal.

Servings: 4
Preparation Time: 15 minutes
Cooking Time: 40 minutes
Ingredients:

- 4 large bell peppers, tops cut off and seeds removed
- 1 cup (185 g) cooked quinoa
- 1/2 cup (75 g) diced tomatoes
- 1/2 cup (75 g) black beans, rinsed and drained
- 1/4 cup (30 g) corn kernels
- 1/4 cup (30 g) chopped onions
- 1/4 cup (30 g) shredded cheese (optional)
- 1 tablespoon (15 ml) olive oil
- 1 teaspoon (5 g) cumin
- Salt and pepper to taste

Instructions:

1. Preheat oven to 375°F (190°C).
2. In a bowl, mix cooked quinoa, diced tomatoes, black beans, corn, onions, olive oil, cumin, salt, and pepper.
3. Stuff each bell pepper with the quinoa mixture and place in a baking dish.
4. Top with shredded cheese if desired.
5. Bake for 35-40 minutes until the peppers are tender and the filling is heated through.
6. Serve hot.

142. Eggplant Parmesan

A healthier version of the classic Italian dish, baked instead of fried.

Servings: 4
Preparation Time: 20 minutes
Cooking Time: 45 minutes
Ingredients:

- 2 large eggplants, sliced into rounds
- 2 cups (480 ml) marinara sauce
- 1 cup (100 g) shredded mozzarella cheese
- 1/2 cup (50 g) grated Parmesan cheese
- 1/2 cup (60 g) whole wheat breadcrumbs
- 1 egg, beaten
- 2 tablespoons (30 ml) olive oil
- 1 teaspoon (5 g) Italian seasoning
- Salt and pepper to taste

Instructions:

1. Preheat oven to 375°F (190°C).
2. Dip eggplant slices in beaten egg, then coat with breadcrumbs.
3. Arrange on a baking sheet and drizzle with olive oil.
4. Bake for 20 minutes until golden brown.
5. Spread a layer of marinara sauce in a baking dish, add a layer of eggplant slices, and top with mozzarella and Parmesan cheese.
6. Repeat layers and top with remaining cheese.
7. Bake for an additional 25 minutes until bubbly and golden.
8. Serve hot.

143. Veggie Stir-Fry

A quick and easy dish that's packed with colorful vegetables and flavor.

Servings: 4
Preparation Time: 10 minutes
Cooking Time: 15 minutes
Ingredients:

- 1 cup (150 g) broccoli florets
- 1 red bell pepper, sliced
- 1 yellow bell pepper, sliced
- 1 carrot, sliced
- 1 zucchini, sliced
- 1 cup (150 g) snap peas
- 2 tablespoons (30 ml) soy sauce
- 1 tablespoon (15 ml) sesame oil
- 1 tablespoon (15 ml) olive oil
- 1 garlic clove, minced
- 1 teaspoon (5 g) ginger, minced

Instructions:

1. Heat olive oil in a large skillet over medium-high heat.
2. Add garlic and ginger, sauté for 1 minute.
3. Add all vegetables and stir-fry for 10-12 minutes until tender.
4. Stir in soy sauce and sesame oil.
5. Serve hot over brown rice or quinoa.

144. Quinoa Salad

A refreshing and protein-packed salad that's perfect for lunch or dinner.

Servings: 4
Preparation Time: 15 minutes
Cooking Time: 15 minutes
Ingredients:

- 1 cup (185 g) quinoa, cooked and cooled
- 1 cup (150 g) cherry tomatoes, halved
- 1 cucumber, diced
- 1/4 cup (30 g) red onion, finely chopped
- 1/4 cup (30 g) feta cheese, crumbled
- 2 tablespoons (30 ml) olive oil
- 1 tablespoon (15 ml) lemon juice
- Salt and pepper to taste

- Fresh parsley for garnish

Instructions:

1. In a large bowl, combine cooked quinoa, cherry tomatoes, cucumber, red onion, and feta cheese.
2. In a small bowl, whisk together olive oil, lemon juice, salt, and pepper.
3. Pour the dressing over the salad and toss to combine.
4. Garnish with fresh parsley and serve immediately.

145. Lentil Soup

A hearty and nutritious soup that's perfect for a comforting meal.

Servings: 4
Preparation Time: 15 minutes
Cooking Time: 40 minutes
Ingredients:

- 1 cup (200 g) dried lentils, rinsed
- 1 onion, diced
- 2 carrots, sliced
- 2 celery stalks, sliced
- 2 garlic cloves, minced
- 1 can (400 g) diced tomatoes
- 4 cups (1 liter) vegetable broth
- 1 teaspoon (5 g) cumin
- 1 teaspoon (5 g) thyme
- Salt and pepper to taste

Instructions:

1. In a large pot, sauté onion, carrots, celery, and garlic until softened.
2. Add lentils, diced tomatoes, vegetable broth, cumin, and thyme.
3. Bring to a boil, then reduce heat and simmer for 30-40 minutes until lentils are tender.
4. Season with salt and pepper.
5. Serve hot.

146. Veggie Burger

A delicious and hearty veggie burger that's perfect for a satisfying meal.

Servings: 4

Preparation Time: 15 minutes

Cooking Time: 10 minutes

Ingredients:

- 1 can (400 g) black beans, rinsed and drained
- 1/2 cup (75 g) breadcrumbs
- 1/4 cup (30 g) finely chopped onion
- 1 garlic clove, minced
- 1 egg
- 1 teaspoon (5 g) cumin
- Salt and pepper to taste
- 2 tablespoons (30 ml) olive oil
- Whole grain burger buns
- Lettuce, tomato, and your favorite burger toppings

Instructions:

1. In a bowl, mash black beans with a fork.
2. Add breadcrumbs, onion, garlic, egg, cumin, salt, and pepper. Mix well.
3. Form the mixture into patties.
4. Heat olive oil in a skillet over medium heat.
5. Cook the patties for 4-5 minutes on each side until golden brown.
6. Serve on whole grain buns with lettuce, tomato, and your favorite toppings.

147. Spinach and Feta Stuffed Mushrooms

Savory mushrooms filled with a delicious spinach and feta mixture.

Servings: 4

Preparation Time: 10 minutes

Cooking Time: 20 minutes

Ingredients:

- 12 large mushrooms, stems removed
- 1 cup (150 g) spinach, chopped
- 1/4 cup (30 g) feta cheese, crumbled
- 2 tablespoons (30 ml) olive oil
- 1 garlic clove, minced
- Salt and pepper to taste

Instructions:

1. Preheat oven to 375°F (190°C).
2. Heat olive oil in a skillet and sauté garlic until fragrant.
3. Add spinach and cook until wilted.
4. Remove from heat and stir in feta cheese, salt, and pepper.
5. Stuff each mushroom cap with the spinach mixture.
6. Arrange mushrooms on a baking sheet and bake for 20 minutes until tender.
7. Serve warm.

148. Cauliflower Steak

A hearty and flavorful dish that makes a perfect vegetarian main course.

Servings: 2

Preparation Time: 10 minutes

Cooking Time: 25 minutes

Ingredients:

- 1 large head of cauliflower, sliced into thick steaks
- 2 tablespoons (30 ml) olive oil
- 1 teaspoon (5 g) garlic powder
- 1 teaspoon (5 g) paprika
- Salt and pepper to taste
- Fresh parsley for garnish

Instructions:

1. Preheat oven to 400°F (200°C).
2. Place cauliflower steaks on a baking sheet and brush with olive oil.
3. Season with garlic powder, paprika, salt, and pepper.
4. Roast for 20-25 minutes until golden brown and tender.
5. Garnish with fresh parsley and serve immediately.

149. Chickpea Curry

A warm and comforting dish that's packed with flavor and protein.

Servings: 4
Preparation Time: 10 minutes
Cooking Time: 30 minutes
Ingredients:

- 2 cups (400 g) canned chickpeas, rinsed and drained
- 1 onion, chopped
- 2 garlic cloves, minced
- 1 tablespoon (15 g) ginger, minced
- 1 can (400 ml) coconut milk
- 1 can (400 g) diced tomatoes
- 2 tablespoons (30 g) curry powder
- 1 teaspoon (5 g) cumin
- 1 teaspoon (5 g) turmeric
- 2 tablespoons (30 ml) olive oil
- Salt and pepper to taste
- Fresh cilantro for garnish

Instructions:

1. Heat olive oil in a large pot over medium heat.
2. Add onion, garlic, and ginger, sauté until softened.
3. Stir in curry powder, cumin, and turmeric, cook for 1 minute.
4. Add chickpeas, coconut milk, and diced tomatoes, bring to a simmer.
5. Cook for 20-25 minutes, stirring occasionally, until the sauce thickens.
6. Season with salt and pepper.
7. Garnish with fresh cilantro and serve hot.

150. Stuffed Zucchini Boats

A healthy and satisfying dish that's perfect for dinner.

Servings: 4
Preparation Time: 15 minutes
Cooking Time: 30 minutes

Ingredients:

- 4 zucchinis, halved lengthwise and seeds removed
- 1 cup (185 g) cooked quinoa
- 1/2 cup (75 g) diced tomatoes
- 1/4 cup (30 g) corn kernels
- 1/4 cup (30 g) black beans, rinsed and drained
- 1/4 cup (30 g) shredded cheese (optional)
- 1 tablespoon (15 ml) olive oil
- 1 teaspoon (5 g) cumin
- Salt and pepper to taste

Instructions:

1. Preheat oven to 375°F (190°C).
2. In a bowl, mix cooked quinoa, diced tomatoes, corn, black beans, olive oil, cumin, salt, and pepper.
3. Stuff each zucchini half with the quinoa mixture and place in a baking dish.
4. Top with shredded cheese if desired.
5. Bake for 25-30 minutes until the zucchinis are tender and the filling is heated through.
6. Serve hot.

151. Grilled Veggie Skewers

A colorful and nutritious dish that's perfect for grilling season.

Servings: 4
Preparation Time: 15 minutes
Cooking Time: 10 minutes
Ingredients:

- 1 red bell pepper, cut into chunks
- 1 yellow bell pepper, cut into chunks
- 1 zucchini, sliced
- 1 red onion, cut into chunks
- 1 cup (150 g) cherry tomatoes
- 2 tablespoons (30 ml) olive oil
- 1 tablespoon (15 ml) balsamic vinegar
- Salt and pepper to taste
- Wooden or metal skewers

Instructions:

1. Preheat grill to medium-high heat.
2. In a bowl, mix olive oil, balsamic vinegar, salt, and pepper.
3. Thread vegetables onto skewers and brush with the olive oil mixture.
4. Grill for 8-10 minutes, turning occasionally, until vegetables are tender and slightly charred.
5. Serve immediately.

152. Black Bean Tacos

A quick and delicious meal that's perfect for a weeknight dinner.

Servings: 4
Preparation Time: 10 minutes
Cooking Time: 10 minutes
Ingredients:

- 1 can (400 g) black beans, rinsed and drained
- 1 teaspoon (5 g) cumin
- 1 teaspoon (5 g) chili powder
- 1 tablespoon (15 ml) olive oil
- Salt and pepper to taste
- 8 small whole grain tortillas
- 1 avocado, sliced
- 1 cup (150 g) shredded lettuce
- 1/2 cup (75 g) diced tomatoes
- Fresh cilantro for garnish

Instructions:

1. Heat olive oil in a skillet over medium heat.
2. Add black beans, cumin, chili powder, salt, and pepper.
3. Cook for 5-7 minutes, stirring occasionally, until heated through.
4. Warm tortillas in a dry skillet or microwave.
5. Fill tortillas with black bean mixture, avocado slices, shredded lettuce, and diced tomatoes.
6. Garnish with fresh cilantro and serve immediately.

153. Ratatouille

A classic French dish that's both hearty and healthy.

Servings: 4
Preparation Time: 15 minutes
Cooking Time: 45 minutes
Ingredients:

- 1 eggplant, diced
- 1 zucchini, sliced
- 1 yellow squash, sliced
- 1 red bell pepper, diced
- 1 onion, chopped
- 2 garlic cloves, minced
- 2 cups (480 ml) tomato sauce
- 2 tablespoons (30 ml) olive oil
- 1 teaspoon (5 g) dried basil
- 1 teaspoon (5 g) dried oregano
- Salt and pepper to taste

Instructions:

1. Preheat oven to 375°F (190°C).
2. In a large oven-safe pot, heat olive oil over medium heat.
3. Add onion and garlic, sauté until softened.
4. Add eggplant, zucchini, yellow squash, and red bell pepper.
5. Cook for 10 minutes, stirring occasionally.
6. Add tomato sauce, basil, oregano, salt, and pepper.
7. Transfer pot to the oven and bake for 30 minutes until vegetables are tender.
8. Serve hot.

154. Veggie Pizza

A delicious and healthy pizza that's perfect for a family meal.

Servings: 4
Preparation Time: 15 minutes
Cooking Time: 15 minutes
Ingredients:

- 1 whole grain pizza crust
- 1/2 cup (120 ml) tomato sauce

- 1 cup (100 g) shredded mozzarella cheese
- 1/2 cup (75 g) sliced mushrooms
- 1/2 cup (75 g) sliced bell peppers
- 1/2 cup (75 g) spinach leaves
- 1/4 cup (30 g) sliced black olives
- 1 tablespoon (15 g) grated Parmesan cheese
- 1 teaspoon (5 g) dried oregano

Instructions:
1. Preheat oven to 450°F (230°C).
2. Spread tomato sauce over the pizza crust.
3. Sprinkle with mozzarella cheese.
4. Arrange mushrooms, bell peppers, spinach leaves, and black olives on top.
5. Sprinkle with Parmesan cheese and dried oregano.
6. Bake for 12-15 minutes until the crust is golden and the cheese is bubbly.
7. Slice and serve hot.

155. Sweet Potato and Black Bean Chili

A hearty and warming dish that's perfect for a nutritious dinner.

Servings: 4
Preparation Time: 15 minutes
Cooking Time: 30 minutes
Ingredients:
- 2 large sweet potatoes, peeled and diced
- 1 can (400 g) black beans, rinsed and drained
- 1 can (400 g) diced tomatoes
- 1 onion, chopped
- 2 garlic cloves, minced
- 2 tablespoons (30 g) chili powder
- 1 teaspoon (5 g) cumin
- 1 teaspoon (5 g) smoked paprika
- 2 cups (480 ml) vegetable broth
- 1 tablespoon (15 ml) olive oil
- Salt and pepper to taste

Instructions:
1. Heat olive oil in a large pot over medium heat.

2. Add onion and garlic, sauté until softened.
3. Stir in chili powder, cumin, and smoked paprika.
4. Add sweet potatoes, black beans, diced tomatoes, and vegetable broth.
5. Bring to a boil, then reduce heat and simmer for 25-30 minutes until sweet potatoes are tender.
6. Season with salt and pepper.
7. Serve hot, garnished with fresh cilantro if desired.

156. Mushroom Stroganoff

A creamy and flavorful dish that's perfect for a comforting meal.

Servings: 4
Preparation Time: 10 minutes
Cooking Time: 20 minutes
Ingredients:
- 1 pound (450 g) mushrooms, sliced
- 1 onion, chopped
- 2 garlic cloves, minced
- 1 cup (240 ml) vegetable broth
- 1/2 cup (120 ml) Greek yogurt
- 1 tablespoon (15 ml) olive oil
- 1 tablespoon (15 g) flour (optional, for thickening)
- 1 teaspoon (5 g) paprika
- Salt and pepper to taste
- Fresh parsley for garnish

Instructions:
1. Heat olive oil in a large skillet over medium heat.
2. Add onion and garlic, sauté until softened.
3. Add mushrooms and cook until they release their moisture and start to brown.
4. Stir in flour (if using) and cook for 1 minute.
5. Add vegetable broth and paprika, bring to a simmer.

6. Reduce heat and stir in Greek yogurt, season with salt and pepper.
7. Cook for an additional 5 minutes until the sauce thickens.
8. Serve hot, garnished with fresh parsley.

157. Veggie Shepherd's Pie
A hearty and comforting dish that's perfect for a family dinner.
Servings: 4
Preparation Time: 20 minutes
Cooking Time: 30 minutes
Ingredients:
- 1 cup (150 g) lentils, cooked
- 2 cups (300 g) mixed vegetables (peas, carrots, corn)
- 1 onion, chopped
- 2 garlic cloves, minced
- 1 cup (240 ml) vegetable broth
- 2 tablespoons (30 ml) tomato paste
- 4 large potatoes, peeled and mashed
- 1/4 cup (60 ml) milk
- 2 tablespoons (30 g) butter
- Salt and pepper to taste

Instructions:
1. Preheat oven to 375°F (190°C).
2. In a skillet, sauté onion and garlic until softened.
3. Add cooked lentils, mixed vegetables, vegetable broth, and tomato paste. Cook until heated through.
4. Spread the lentil mixture in a baking dish.
5. In a bowl, mix mashed potatoes with milk and butter, season with salt and pepper.
6. Spread mashed potatoes over the lentil mixture.
7. Bake for 20-25 minutes until the top is golden brown.
8. Serve hot.

158. Roasted Butternut Squash
A simple and delicious side dish that's packed with flavor.
Servings: 4
Preparation Time: 10 minutes
Cooking Time: 25 minutes
Ingredients:
- 1 large butternut squash, peeled and cubed
- 2 tablespoons (30 ml) olive oil
- 1 teaspoon (5 g) cinnamon
- Salt and pepper to taste

Instructions:
1. Preheat oven to 400°F (200°C).
2. In a bowl, toss butternut squash cubes with olive oil, cinnamon, salt, and pepper.
3. Spread on a baking sheet in a single layer.
4. Roast for 20-25 minutes until tender and caramelized.
5. Serve hot.

159. Spinach and Ricotta Stuffed Shells
A flavorful and satisfying dish that's perfect for a hearty meal.
Servings: 4
Preparation Time: 20 minutes
Cooking Time: 30 minutes
Ingredients:
- 12 large pasta shells
- 1 cup (240 g) ricotta cheese
- 1 cup (150 g) spinach, chopped
- 1/2 cup (50 g) grated Parmesan cheese
- 2 cups (480 ml) marinara sauce
- 1 egg, beaten
- Salt and pepper to taste

Instructions:
1. Preheat oven to 375°F (190°C).
2. Cook pasta shells according to package instructions, drain and set aside.
3. In a bowl, mix ricotta cheese, spinach, Parmesan cheese, egg, salt, and pepper.

4. Fill each pasta shell with the ricotta mixture.
5. Spread half of the marinara sauce in a baking dish.
6. Arrange stuffed shells on top of the sauce and cover with remaining sauce.
7. Bake for 25-30 minutes until bubbly and heated through.
8. Serve hot.

160. Grilled Portobello Mushrooms

A simple and flavorful dish that's perfect for a light meal or side dish.

Servings: 4
Preparation Time: 10 minutes
Cooking Time: 10 minutes
Ingredients:

*   4 large portobello mushrooms
*   2 tablespoons (30 ml) olive oil
*   2 tablespoons (30 ml) balsamic vinegar
*   1 garlic clove, minced
*   Salt and pepper to taste
*   Fresh parsley for garnish

Instructions:

1. Preheat grill to medium-high heat.
2. In a small bowl, mix olive oil, balsamic vinegar, garlic, salt, and pepper.
3. Brush the mushroom caps with the olive oil mixture.
4. Grill mushrooms for 5-6 minutes on each side until tender.
5. Garnish with fresh parsley and serve immediately.

Chapter 14: Perfect Poultry

Poultry is a versatile and lean source of protein that fits perfectly into a diabetes-friendly diet. With the right recipes, you can enjoy a variety of delicious and healthy chicken and turkey dishes that are both satisfying and nutritious. This chapter offers a selection of perfect poultry recipes that are flavorful and easy to prepare.

161. Baked Chicken Breast
A simple and healthy dish that's perfect for any meal.
Servings: 4
Preparation Time: 10 minutes
Cooking Time: 25 minutes
Ingredients:
- 4 boneless, skinless chicken breasts
- 2 tablespoons (30 ml) olive oil
- 1 teaspoon (5 g) garlic powder
- 1 teaspoon (5 g) paprika
- Salt and pepper to taste
- Fresh parsley for garnish

Instructions:
1. Preheat oven to 375°F (190°C).
2. Rub chicken breasts with olive oil and season with garlic powder, paprika, salt, and pepper.
3. Place chicken on a baking sheet and bake for 20-25 minutes until cooked through.
4. Garnish with fresh parsley and serve immediately.

162. Grilled Turkey Burgers
A healthy and delicious alternative to traditional beef burgers.
Servings: 4
Preparation Time: 10 minutes
Cooking Time: 10 minutes
Ingredients:
- 1 pound (450 g) ground turkey
- 1/4 cup (30 g) breadcrumbs
- 1 egg
- 1 garlic clove, minced
- 1 teaspoon (5 g) Italian seasoning
- Salt and pepper to taste
- Whole grain burger buns
- Lettuce, tomato, and your favorite burger toppings

Instructions:
1. Preheat grill to medium-high heat.
2. In a bowl, mix ground turkey, breadcrumbs, egg, garlic, Italian seasoning, salt, and pepper.
3. Form the mixture into patties.
4. Grill patties for 5-6 minutes on each side until fully cooked.
5. Serve on whole grain buns with your favorite toppings.

163. Chicken Stir-Fry
A quick and easy dish that's packed with vegetables and flavor.
Servings: 4
Preparation Time: 10 minutes
Cooking Time: 15 minutes
Ingredients:
- 1 pound (450 g) chicken breast, sliced
- 2 tablespoons (30 ml) soy sauce
- 1 tablespoon (15 ml) sesame oil
- 1 red bell pepper, sliced
- 1 green bell pepper, sliced
- 1 cup (150 g) snap peas
- 1 carrot, sliced
- 1 garlic clove, minced
- 1 teaspoon (5 g) ginger, minced

Instructions:
1. Heat sesame oil in a large skillet over medium-high heat.
2. Add garlic and ginger, sauté for 1 minute.
3. Add chicken and cook until browned.

4. Add bell peppers, snap peas, and carrot. Stir-fry for 5-7 minutes.
5. Stir in soy sauce and cook for another 2 minutes.
6. Serve hot over brown rice or quinoa.

164. Lemon Garlic Chicken

A flavorful and aromatic dish that's perfect for a weeknight dinner.

Servings: 4
Preparation Time: 10 minutes
Cooking Time: 30 minutes
Ingredients:

- 4 chicken breasts
- 2 tablespoons (30 ml) olive oil
- Juice of 1 lemon
- 4 garlic cloves, minced
- 1 teaspoon (5 g) dried oregano
- Salt and pepper to taste

Instructions:

1. Preheat oven to 375°F (190°C).
2. In a bowl, mix olive oil, lemon juice, garlic, oregano, salt, and pepper.
3. Place chicken breasts in a baking dish and pour the mixture over them.
4. Bake for 25-30 minutes until the chicken is cooked through.
5. Serve hot with your favorite side dish.

165. Turkey Meatloaf

A lighter version of the classic meatloaf that's just as delicious.

Servings: 6
Preparation Time: 15 minutes
Cooking Time: 45 minutes
Ingredients:

- 1 pound (450 g) ground turkey
- 1/2 cup (75 g) breadcrumbs
- 1/4 cup (30 g) finely chopped onion
- 1 egg
- 2 tablespoons (30 ml) ketchup
- 1 tablespoon (15 ml) Worcestershire sauce
- 1 garlic clove, minced
- Salt and pepper to taste

Instructions:

1. Preheat oven to 375°F (190°C).
2. In a bowl, mix ground turkey, breadcrumbs, onion, egg, ketchup, Worcestershire sauce, garlic, salt, and pepper.
3. Form the mixture into a loaf and place in a baking dish.
4. Bake for 40-45 minutes until cooked through.
5. Serve hot with your favorite side dish.

166. Chicken Parmesan

A healthier take on the classic Italian dish, baked instead of fried.

Servings: 4
Preparation Time: 15 minutes
Cooking Time: 30 minutes
Ingredients:

- 4 chicken breasts
- 1 cup (100 g) breadcrumbs
- 1/2 cup (50 g) grated Parmesan cheese
- 1 cup (240 ml) marinara sauce
- 1 cup (100 g) shredded mozzarella cheese
- 1 egg, beaten
- 2 tablespoons (30 ml) olive oil

Instructions:

1. Preheat oven to 375°F (190°C).
2. In a bowl, mix breadcrumbs and Parmesan cheese.
3. Dip chicken breasts in beaten egg, then coat with breadcrumb mixture.
4. Heat olive oil in a skillet over medium heat and brown chicken breasts on both sides.
5. Place chicken in a baking dish, top with marinara sauce and mozzarella cheese.
6. Bake for 20-25 minutes until the cheese is melted and bubbly.
7. Serve hot.

167. Stuffed Chicken Breast

Juicy chicken breasts stuffed with a flavorful spinach and cheese mixture.

Servings: 4
Preparation Time: 15 minutes
Cooking Time: 25 minutes
Ingredients:

- 4 chicken breasts
- 1 cup (150 g) spinach, chopped
- 1/2 cup (50 g) shredded mozzarella cheese
- 1/4 cup (30 g) grated Parmesan cheese
- 1 garlic clove, minced
- 2 tablespoons (30 ml) olive oil
- Salt and pepper to taste

Instructions:

1. Preheat oven to 375°F (190°C).
2. In a bowl, mix spinach, mozzarella cheese, Parmesan cheese, and garlic.
3. Cut a pocket into each chicken breast and stuff with the spinach mixture.
4. Secure with toothpicks if necessary.
5. Heat olive oil in a skillet over medium heat and brown chicken breasts on both sides.
6. Transfer to a baking dish and bake for 20-25 minutes until cooked through.
7. Serve hot.

168. BBQ Chicken Skewers

Tender and flavorful chicken skewers perfect for grilling.

Servings: 4
Preparation Time: 10 minutes
Cooking Time: 10 minutes
Ingredients:

- 1 pound (450 g) chicken breast, cut into cubes
- 1/2 cup (120 ml) BBQ sauce
- 2 tablespoons (30 ml) olive oil
- Salt and pepper to taste
- Wooden or metal skewers

Instructions:

1. Preheat grill to medium-high heat.
2. In a bowl, mix chicken cubes with BBQ sauce, olive oil, salt, and pepper.
3. Thread chicken onto skewers.
4. Grill for 8-10 minutes, turning occasionally, until chicken is cooked through.
5. Serve immediately.

169. Chicken Fajitas

A colorful and flavorful dish that's quick to prepare and perfect for a healthy meal.

Servings: 4
Preparation Time: 10 minutes
Cooking Time: 15 minutes
Ingredients:

- 1 pound (450 g) chicken breast, sliced
- 1 red bell pepper, sliced
- 1 green bell pepper, sliced
- 1 onion, sliced
- 2 tablespoons (30 ml) olive oil
- 2 tablespoons (30 g) fajita seasoning
- Whole wheat tortillas
- Fresh cilantro, chopped
- Lime wedges

Instructions:

1. Heat olive oil in a large skillet over medium-high heat.
2. Add chicken slices and cook until browned.
3. Add bell peppers and onion, sauté until tender.
4. Sprinkle fajita seasoning over the chicken and vegetables, stir to coat evenly.
5. Serve the fajita mixture in whole wheat tortillas, garnished with fresh cilantro and a squeeze of lime.

170. Roasted Turkey Breast

A simple and elegant dish that's perfect for a nutritious dinner.

Servings: 6
Preparation Time: 15 minutes
Cooking Time: 1 hour 30 minutes
Ingredients:

- 1 boneless turkey breast (about 3 pounds/1.4 kg)
- 2 tablespoons (30 ml) olive oil
- 4 garlic cloves, minced
- 1 tablespoon (15 g) fresh rosemary, chopped
- 1 tablespoon (15 g) fresh thyme, chopped
- Salt and pepper to taste

Instructions:

1. Preheat oven to 375°F (190°C).
2. In a small bowl, mix olive oil, garlic, rosemary, thyme, salt, and pepper.
3. Rub the mixture all over the turkey breast.
4. Place the turkey breast on a roasting pan and roast for 1 hour 30 minutes, or until the internal temperature reaches 165°F (74°C).
5. Let the turkey rest for 10 minutes before slicing and serving.

171. Chicken Curry

A warm and comforting dish that's full of flavor and spices.

Servings: 4
Preparation Time: 15 minutes
Cooking Time: 30 minutes
Ingredients:

- 1 pound (450 g) chicken breast, cubed
- 1 onion, chopped
- 2 garlic cloves, minced
- 1 tablespoon (15 g) ginger, minced
- 1 can (400 ml) coconut milk
- 1 can (400 g) diced tomatoes
- 2 tablespoons (30 g) curry powder
- 1 teaspoon (5 g) cumin
- 1 teaspoon (5 g) turmeric
- 2 tablespoons (30 ml) olive oil
- Salt and pepper to taste
- Fresh cilantro for garnish

Instructions:

1. Heat olive oil in a large pot over medium heat.
2. Add onion, garlic, and ginger, sauté until softened.
3. Stir in curry powder, cumin, and turmeric, cook for 1 minute.
4. Add chicken cubes and cook until browned.
5. Pour in coconut milk and diced tomatoes, bring to a simmer.
6. Cook for 20-25 minutes, stirring occasionally, until the chicken is cooked through and the sauce thickens.
7. Season with salt and pepper, garnish with fresh cilantro, and serve hot.

172. Greek Lemon Chicken

A zesty and aromatic dish that's perfect for a Mediterranean-inspired meal.

Servings: 4
Preparation Time: 10 minutes
Cooking Time: 25 minutes
Ingredients:

- 4 chicken breasts
- 1/4 cup (60 ml) olive oil
- Juice of 2 lemons
- 4 garlic cloves, minced
- 1 tablespoon (15 g) dried oregano
- Salt and pepper to taste
- Fresh parsley for garnish

Instructions:

1. Preheat oven to 375°F (190°C).
2. In a bowl, mix olive oil, lemon juice, garlic, oregano, salt, and pepper.
3. Place chicken breasts in a baking dish and pour the lemon mixture over them.

4. Bake for 25-30 minutes until the chicken is cooked through.
5. Garnish with fresh parsley and serve immediately.

173. Honey Mustard Chicken

A sweet and tangy dish that's easy to prepare and full of flavor.

Servings: 4
Preparation Time: 10 minutes
Cooking Time: 25 minutes
Ingredients:

- 4 chicken breasts
- 1/4 cup (60 ml) Dijon mustard
- 1/4 cup (60 ml) honey
- 2 tablespoons (30 ml) olive oil
- 1 garlic clove, minced
- Salt and pepper to taste

Instructions:

1. Preheat oven to 375°F (190°C).
2. In a bowl, mix Dijon mustard, honey, olive oil, garlic, salt, and pepper.
3. Place chicken breasts in a baking dish and brush with the honey mustard mixture.
4. Bake for 25-30 minutes until the chicken is cooked through.
5. Serve hot.

174. Spicy Chicken Wings

These wings are baked to perfection and coated in a deliciously spicy sauce.

Servings: 4
Preparation Time: 10 minutes
Cooking Time: 40 minutes
Ingredients:

- 1 pound (450 g) chicken wings
- 2 tablespoons (30 ml) olive oil
- 1/4 cup (60 ml) hot sauce
- 1 tablespoon (15 g) butter, melted
- 1 teaspoon (5 g) garlic powder
- Salt and pepper to taste

Instructions:

1. Preheat oven to 400°F (200°C).
2. Toss chicken wings with olive oil, garlic powder, salt, and pepper.
3. Arrange wings on a baking sheet and bake for 35-40 minutes until crispy.
4. In a bowl, mix hot sauce and melted butter.
5. Toss the baked wings in the sauce.
6. Serve immediately.

175. Chicken Tacos

A quick and tasty dish that's perfect for a weeknight meal.

Servings: 4
Preparation Time: 10 minutes
Cooking Time: 15 minutes
Ingredients:

- 1 pound (450 g) chicken breast, diced
- 1 tablespoon (15 ml) olive oil
- 1 tablespoon (15 g) taco seasoning
- 8 small whole wheat tortillas
- 1 cup (150 g) shredded lettuce
- 1/2 cup (75 g) diced tomatoes
- 1/2 cup (60 g) shredded cheese
- Fresh cilantro, chopped

Instructions:

1. Heat olive oil in a skillet over medium heat.
2. Add chicken and taco seasoning, cook until the chicken is browned and cooked through.
3. Warm tortillas in a dry skillet or microwave.
4. Fill tortillas with cooked chicken, shredded lettuce, diced tomatoes, shredded cheese, and fresh cilantro.
5. Serve immediately.

176. Herb-Crusted Chicken

A flavorful and crispy chicken dish that's easy to make and delicious.

Servings: 4
Preparation Time: 10 minutes
Cooking Time: 25 minutes
Ingredients:

- 4 chicken breasts
- 1/2 cup (50 g) breadcrumbs
- 1/4 cup (30 g) grated Parmesan cheese
- 2 tablespoons (30 g) fresh parsley, chopped
- 2 garlic cloves, minced
- 2 tablespoons (30 ml) olive oil
- Salt and pepper to taste

Instructions:

1. Preheat oven to 375°F (190°C).
2. In a bowl, mix breadcrumbs, Parmesan cheese, parsley, garlic, salt, and pepper.
3. Brush chicken breasts with olive oil and press the breadcrumb mixture onto them.
4. Place chicken on a baking sheet and bake for 20-25 minutes until the chicken is cooked through and the crust is golden brown.
5. Serve hot.

177. Chicken and Veggie Kebabs

These colorful and nutritious kebabs are perfect for grilling and full of flavor.

Servings: 4
Preparation Time: 15 minutes
Cooking Time: 10 minutes
Ingredients:

- 1 pound (450 g) chicken breast, cut into cubes
- 1 red bell pepper, cut into chunks
- 1 yellow bell pepper, cut into chunks
- 1 zucchini, sliced
- 1 red onion, cut into chunks
- 2 tablespoons (30 ml) olive oil
- 1 tablespoon (15 ml) lemon juice

- 1 teaspoon (5 g) garlic powder
- Salt and pepper to taste
- Wooden or metal skewers

Instructions:

1. Preheat grill to medium-high heat.
2. In a bowl, mix olive oil, lemon juice, garlic powder, salt, and pepper.
3. Thread chicken and vegetables onto skewers.
4. Brush with the olive oil mixture.
5. Grill for 8-10 minutes, turning occasionally, until chicken is cooked through and vegetables are tender.
6. Serve immediately.

178. Teriyaki Chicken

A delicious and savory dish that's perfect for a quick and healthy meal.

Servings: 4
Preparation Time: 10 minutes
Cooking Time: 15 minutes
Ingredients:

- 1 pound (450 g) chicken breast, sliced
- 1/4 cup (60 ml) soy sauce
- 2 tablespoons (30 ml) honey
- 2 tablespoons (30 ml) rice vinegar
- 1 tablespoon (15 ml) sesame oil
- 2 garlic cloves, minced
- 1 teaspoon (5 g) ginger, minced
- 1 teaspoon (5 g) cornstarch
- 2 tablespoons (30 ml) water
- Sesame seeds for garnish
- Green onions for garnish

Instructions:

1. In a bowl, mix soy sauce, honey, rice vinegar, sesame oil, garlic, and ginger.
2. Heat a large skillet over medium-high heat and add chicken slices.
3. Pour the soy sauce mixture over the chicken and cook until the chicken is browned and cooked through.

4. Mix cornstarch and water in a small bowl, then add to the skillet to thicken the sauce.
5. Cook for an additional 2 minutes until the sauce thickens.
6. Garnish with sesame seeds and green onions before serving.

179. Buffalo Chicken Lettuce Wraps

A spicy and refreshing dish that's perfect for a light meal or appetizer.
Servings: 4
Preparation Time: 10 minutes
Cooking Time: 10 minutes
Ingredients:

- 1 pound (450 g) chicken breast, diced
- 1/4 cup (60 ml) hot sauce
- 1 tablespoon (15 g) butter
- 1 teaspoon (5 g) garlic powder
- 1 head of lettuce, leaves separated
- 1/4 cup (60 g) blue cheese crumbles
- 1/4 cup (60 ml) ranch dressing (optional)
- Salt and pepper to taste

Instructions:

1. Heat a skillet over medium heat and add butter.
2. Add diced chicken and cook until browned and cooked through.
3. Stir in hot sauce and garlic powder, cook for an additional 2 minutes.
4. Season with salt and pepper.
5. Serve chicken in lettuce leaves, topped with blue cheese crumbles and a drizzle of ranch dressing if desired.

180. Balsamic Glazed Chicken

A flavorful and elegant dish that's perfect for a special dinner.
Servings: 4
Preparation Time: 10 minutes
Cooking Time: 25 minutes
Ingredients:

- 4 chicken breasts
- 1/4 cup (60 ml) balsamic vinegar
- 2 tablespoons (30 ml) olive oil
- 2 garlic cloves, minced
- 1 tablespoon (15 ml) honey
- 1 teaspoon (5 g) dried thyme
- Salt and pepper to taste
- Fresh parsley for garnish

Instructions:

1. Preheat oven to 375°F (190°C).
2. In a bowl, mix balsamic vinegar, olive oil, garlic, honey, thyme, salt, and pepper.
3. Place chicken breasts in a baking dish and pour the balsamic mixture over them.
4. Bake for 25-30 minutes until the chicken is cooked through and the glaze is thickened.
5. Garnish with fresh parsley and serve immediately.

Chapter 15: Savory Soups and Stews

Soups and stews are comforting and nourishing meals that are perfect for any time of the year. They can be packed with vegetables, proteins, and flavorful broths, making them ideal for managing diabetes while enjoying hearty and satisfying dishes. This chapter offers a variety of savory soups and stews that are both delicious and diabetes-friendly.

181. Chicken Noodle Soup

A classic and comforting soup that's perfect for a cozy meal.

Servings: 4
Preparation Time: 10 minutes
Cooking Time: 30 minutes
Ingredients:

- 1 pound (450 g) chicken breast, cubed
- 1 onion, chopped
- 2 carrots, sliced
- 2 celery stalks, sliced
- 4 cups (1 liter) chicken broth
- 1 cup (150 g) whole wheat noodles
- 1 tablespoon (15 ml) olive oil
- 1 teaspoon (5 g) dried thyme
- Salt and pepper to taste
- Fresh parsley for garnish

Instructions:

1. Heat olive oil in a large pot over medium heat.
2. Add onion, carrots, and celery, sauté until softened.
3. Add cubed chicken and cook until browned.
4. Pour in chicken broth and bring to a boil.
5. Add whole wheat noodles and dried thyme, reduce heat and simmer for 15 minutes.
6. Season with salt and pepper.
7. Garnish with fresh parsley and serve hot.

182. Lentil Stew

A hearty and nutritious stew that's perfect for a filling meal.

Servings: 4
Preparation Time: 10 minutes
Cooking Time: 40 minutes
Ingredients:

- 1 cup (200 g) dried lentils, rinsed
- 1 onion, chopped
- 2 carrots, sliced
- 2 celery stalks, sliced
- 2 garlic cloves, minced
- 1 can (400 g) diced tomatoes
- 4 cups (1 liter) vegetable broth
- 1 teaspoon (5 g) cumin
- 1 teaspoon (5 g) thyme
- 2 tablespoons (30 ml) olive oil
- Salt and pepper to taste

Instructions:

1. Heat olive oil in a large pot over medium heat.
2. Add onion, carrots, celery, and garlic, sauté until softened.
3. Add lentils, diced tomatoes, vegetable broth, cumin, and thyme.
4. Bring to a boil, then reduce heat and simmer for 30-40 minutes until lentils are tender.
5. Season with salt and pepper.
6. Serve hot.

183. Beef and Vegetable Soup

A flavorful and filling soup that's perfect for a hearty meal.

Servings: 4
Preparation Time: 10 minutes
Cooking Time: 45 minutes
Ingredients:

- 1 pound (450 g) beef stew meat, cubed

- 1 onion, chopped
- 2 carrots, sliced
- 2 potatoes, diced
- 2 celery stalks, sliced
- 4 cups (1 liter) beef broth
- 1 can (400 g) diced tomatoes
- 2 tablespoons (30 ml) olive oil
- 1 teaspoon (5 g) dried thyme
- Salt and pepper to taste

Instructions:
1. Heat olive oil in a large pot over medium heat.
2. Add beef stew meat and cook until browned.
3. Add onion, carrots, potatoes, and celery, sauté until softened.
4. Pour in beef broth and diced tomatoes, bring to a boil.
5. Add dried thyme, reduce heat and simmer for 35-40 minutes until vegetables and beef are tender.
6. Season with salt and pepper.
7. Serve hot.

184. Tomato Basil Soup

A creamy and delicious soup that's perfect for a light meal.

Servings: 4
Preparation Time: 10 minutes
Cooking Time: 25 minutes
Ingredients:
- 1 onion, chopped
- 2 garlic cloves, minced
- 2 cans (800 g) diced tomatoes
- 4 cups (1 liter) vegetable broth
- 1/2 cup (120 ml) heavy cream
- 1/4 cup (15 g) fresh basil, chopped
- 2 tablespoons (30 ml) olive oil
- Salt and pepper to taste

Instructions:
1. Heat olive oil in a large pot over medium heat.

2. Add onion and garlic, sauté until softened.
3. Add diced tomatoes and vegetable broth, bring to a boil.
4. Reduce heat and simmer for 15 minutes.
5. Use an immersion blender to blend the soup until smooth.
6. Stir in heavy cream and fresh basil.
7. Season with salt and pepper.
8. Serve hot.

185. Turkey Chili

A hearty and spicy chili that's perfect for a warming meal.

Servings: 4
Preparation Time: 10 minutes
Cooking Time: 30 minutes
Ingredients:
- 1 pound (450 g) ground turkey
- 1 onion, chopped
- 2 garlic cloves, minced
- 1 bell pepper, chopped
- 1 can (400 g) kidney beans, rinsed and drained
- 1 can (400 g) diced tomatoes
- 2 tablespoons (30 g) chili powder
- 1 teaspoon (5 g) cumin
- 1 teaspoon (5 g) paprika
- 2 tablespoons (30 ml) olive oil
- Salt and pepper to taste

Instructions:
1. Heat olive oil in a large pot over medium heat.
2. Add onion, garlic, and bell pepper, sauté until softened.
3. Add ground turkey and cook until browned.
4. Stir in chili powder, cumin, and paprika.
5. Add kidney beans and diced tomatoes, bring to a boil.
6. Reduce heat and simmer for 20 minutes.
7. Season with salt and pepper.
8. Serve hot.

186. Broccoli Cheddar Soup

A creamy and cheesy soup that's perfect for a comforting meal.

Servings: 4
Preparation Time: 10 minutes
Cooking Time: 25 minutes
Ingredients:

- 1 head of broccoli, chopped
- 1 onion, chopped
- 2 garlic cloves, minced
- 2 cups (480 ml) vegetable broth
- 2 cups (240 ml) milk
- 1 cup (100 g) shredded cheddar cheese
- 2 tablespoons (30 g) butter
- 2 tablespoons (30 g) flour
- Salt and pepper to taste

Instructions:

1. Melt butter in a large pot over medium heat.
2. Add onion and garlic, sauté until softened.
3. Stir in flour and cook for 1 minute.
4. Gradually add vegetable broth and milk, stirring constantly.
5. Add chopped broccoli, bring to a boil, then reduce heat and simmer for 15 minutes.
6. Stir in shredded cheddar cheese until melted.
7. Season with salt and pepper.
8. Serve hot.

187. Butternut Squash Soup

A smooth and velvety soup that's perfect for a healthy and delicious meal.

Servings: 4
Preparation Time: 10 minutes
Cooking Time: 30 minutes
Ingredients:

- 1 large butternut squash, peeled and cubed
- 1 onion, chopped
- 2 garlic cloves, minced
- 4 cups (1 liter) vegetable broth
- 1/2 cup (120 ml) coconut milk
- 2 tablespoons (30 ml) olive oil
- 1 teaspoon (5 g) ground nutmeg
- Salt and pepper to taste

Instructions:

1. Heat olive oil in a large pot over medium heat.
2. Add onion and garlic, sauté until softened.
3. Add butternut squash and vegetable broth, bring to a boil.
4. Reduce heat and simmer for 20-25 minutes until the squash is tender.
5. Use an immersion blender to blend the soup until smooth.
6. Stir in coconut milk and ground nutmeg.
7. Season with salt and pepper.
8. Serve hot.

188. Chicken Tortilla Soup

A spicy and flavorful soup that's perfect for a hearty meal.

Servings: 4
Preparation Time: 10 minutes
Cooking Time: 30 minutes
Ingredients:

- 1 pound (450 g) chicken breast, cubed
- 1 onion, chopped
- 2 garlic cloves, minced
- 1 bell pepper, chopped
- 1 can (400 g) diced tomatoes
- 4 cups (1 liter) chicken broth
- 1 cup (150 g) corn kernels
- 1 teaspoon (5 g) cumin
- 1 teaspoon (5 g) chili powder
- 2 tablespoons (30 ml) olive oil
- Salt and pepper to taste
- Tortilla chips, for serving
- Fresh cilantro, for garnish

Instructions:

1. Heat olive oil in a large pot over medium heat.

2. Add onion, garlic, and bell pepper, sauté until softened.
3. Add chicken and cook until browned.
4. Stir in cumin and chili powder.
5. Add diced tomatoes, chicken broth, and corn, bring to a boil.
6. Reduce heat and simmer for 20 minutes.
7. Season with salt and pepper.
8. Serve hot, topped with tortilla chips and fresh cilantro.

189. Minestrone Soup

A hearty Italian soup packed with vegetables and beans, perfect for a nutritious meal.
Servings: 4
Preparation Time: 15 minutes
Cooking Time: 30 minutes
Ingredients:

- 1 onion, chopped
- 2 carrots, sliced
- 2 celery stalks, sliced
- 1 zucchini, diced
- 1 cup (150 g) green beans, chopped
- 1 can (400 g) diced tomatoes
- 4 cups (1 liter) vegetable broth
- 1 can (400 g) kidney beans, rinsed and drained
- 1 cup (150 g) small pasta
- 2 tablespoons (30 ml) olive oil
- 1 teaspoon (5 g) dried basil
- Salt and pepper to taste
- Fresh parsley for garnish

Instructions:

1. Heat olive oil in a large pot over medium heat.
2. Add onion, carrots, and celery, sauté until softened.
3. Add zucchini, green beans, diced tomatoes, and vegetable broth.
4. Bring to a boil, then reduce heat and simmer for 20 minutes.
5. Stir in kidney beans and pasta, cook until pasta is tender.

6. Season with basil, salt, and pepper.
7. Garnish with fresh parsley and serve hot.

190. Clam Chowder

A creamy and hearty chowder that's perfect for a comforting meal.
Servings: 4
Preparation Time: 10 minutes
Cooking Time: 20 minutes
Ingredients:

- 2 cans (280 g each) clams, drained and juice reserved
- 1 onion, chopped
- 2 celery stalks, sliced
- 2 potatoes, diced
- 2 cups (480 ml) clam juice (from cans)
- 2 cups (480 ml) milk
- 1 cup (240 ml) heavy cream
- 2 tablespoons (30 g) butter
- 2 tablespoons (30 g) flour
- Salt and pepper to taste
- Fresh parsley for garnish

Instructions:

1. Melt butter in a large pot over medium heat.
2. Add onion and celery, sauté until softened.
3. Stir in flour and cook for 1 minute.
4. Gradually add clam juice and milk, stirring constantly.
5. Add potatoes and bring to a boil, then reduce heat and simmer until potatoes are tender.
6. Stir in clams and heavy cream, cook until heated through.
7. Season with salt and pepper.
8. Garnish with fresh parsley and serve hot.

191. Vegetable Stew

A rich and flavorful stew that's perfect for a filling vegetarian meal.

Servings: 4
Preparation Time: 15 minutes
Cooking Time: 40 minutes
Ingredients:

- 1 onion, chopped
- 2 carrots, sliced
- 2 potatoes, diced
- 1 zucchini, sliced
- 1 can (400 g) diced tomatoes
- 4 cups (1 liter) vegetable broth
- 1 cup (150 g) green beans, chopped
- 2 garlic cloves, minced
- 2 tablespoons (30 ml) olive oil
- 1 teaspoon (5 g) dried thyme
- Salt and pepper to taste
- Fresh parsley for garnish

Instructions:

1. Heat olive oil in a large pot over medium heat.
2. Add onion, carrots, potatoes, zucchini, and garlic, sauté until softened.
3. Add diced tomatoes and vegetable broth, bring to a boil.
4. Reduce heat and simmer for 30 minutes until vegetables are tender.
5. Add green beans and cook for an additional 10 minutes.
6. Season with thyme, salt, and pepper.
7. Garnish with fresh parsley and serve hot.

192. French Onion Soup

A classic French soup with caramelized onions and a rich, savory broth.

Servings: 4
Preparation Time: 15 minutes
Cooking Time: 40 minutes
Ingredients:

- 4 large onions, thinly sliced
- 4 cups (1 liter) beef broth
- 2 tablespoons (30 g) butter
- 1 tablespoon (15 ml) olive oil
- 1/2 cup (120 ml) dry white wine
- 1 teaspoon (5 g) thyme
- Salt and pepper to taste
- 4 slices whole grain baguette
- 1 cup (100 g) shredded Gruyere cheese

Instructions:

1. Heat butter and olive oil in a large pot over medium heat.
2. Add onions and cook, stirring frequently, until caramelized (about 25 minutes).
3. Add white wine and cook for 5 minutes.
4. Stir in beef broth and thyme, bring to a boil, then reduce heat and simmer for 15 minutes.
5. Season with salt and pepper.
6. Preheat broiler. Ladle soup into oven-safe bowls, top with baguette slices and shredded cheese.
7. Broil until cheese is melted and bubbly.
8. Serve hot.

193. Chicken and Rice Soup

A comforting and hearty soup that's perfect for a satisfying meal.

Servings: 4
Preparation Time: 10 minutes
Cooking Time: 30 minutes
Ingredients:

- 1 pound (450 g) chicken breast, cubed
- 1 onion, chopped
- 2 carrots, sliced
- 2 celery stalks, sliced
- 1 cup (200 g) cooked brown rice
- 4 cups (1 liter) chicken broth
- 2 tablespoons (30 ml) olive oil
- 1 teaspoon (5 g) dried thyme
- Salt and pepper to taste

Instructions:

1. Heat olive oil in a large pot over medium heat.

2. Add onion, carrots, and celery, sauté until softened.
3. Add cubed chicken and cook until browned.
4. Pour in chicken broth and bring to a boil.
5. Reduce heat and simmer for 20 minutes until chicken is cooked through.
6. Stir in cooked brown rice and thyme.
7. Season with salt and pepper.
8. Serve hot.

194. Black Bean Soup

A flavorful and protein-packed soup that's perfect for a nutritious meal.

Servings: 4
Preparation Time: 10 minutes
Cooking Time: 30 minutes
Ingredients:

- 1 onion, chopped
- 2 garlic cloves, minced
- 1 bell pepper, chopped
- 2 cans (800 g) black beans, rinsed and drained
- 1 can (400 g) diced tomatoes
- 4 cups (1 liter) vegetable broth
- 2 tablespoons (30 ml) olive oil
- 1 teaspoon (5 g) cumin
- 1 teaspoon (5 g) chili powder
- Salt and pepper to taste
- Fresh cilantro for garnish

Instructions:

1. Heat olive oil in a large pot over medium heat.
2. Add onion, garlic, and bell pepper, sauté until softened.
3. Stir in cumin and chili powder, cook for 1 minute.
4. Add black beans, diced tomatoes, and vegetable broth, bring to a boil.
5. Reduce heat and simmer for 20-25 minutes.

6. Use an immersion blender to partially blend the soup, leaving some chunks for texture.
7. Season with salt and pepper.
8. Garnish with fresh cilantro and serve hot.

195. Zucchini Soup

A light and refreshing soup that's perfect for a healthy meal.

Servings: 4
Preparation Time: 10 minutes
Cooking Time: 20 minutes
Ingredients:

- 4 zucchinis, sliced
- 1 onion, chopped
- 2 garlic cloves, minced
- 4 cups (1 liter) vegetable broth
- 1/2 cup (120 ml) heavy cream
- 2 tablespoons (30 ml) olive oil
- Salt and pepper to taste
- Fresh basil for garnish

Instructions:

1. Heat olive oil in a large pot over medium heat.
2. Add onion and garlic, sauté until softened.
3. Add sliced zucchinis and vegetable broth, bring to a boil.
4. Reduce heat and simmer for 15 minutes until zucchinis are tender.
5. Use an immersion blender to blend the soup until smooth.
6. Stir in heavy cream.
7. Season with salt and pepper.
8. Garnish with fresh basil and serve hot.

196. Split Pea Soup

A hearty and satisfying soup that's perfect for a warming meal.

Servings: 4
Preparation Time: 10 minutes
Cooking Time: 45 minutes

Ingredients:
- 1 cup (200 g) dried split peas, rinsed
- 1 onion, chopped
- 2 carrots, sliced
- 2 celery stalks, sliced
- 2 garlic cloves, minced
- 4 cups (1 liter) vegetable broth
- 1 teaspoon (5 g) dried thyme
- 2 tablespoons (30 ml) olive oil
- Salt and pepper to taste

Instructions:
1. Heat olive oil in a large pot over medium heat.
2. Add onion, carrots, celery, and garlic, sauté until softened.
3. Add split peas, vegetable broth, and thyme, bring to a boil.
4. Reduce heat and simmer for 35-40 minutes until peas are tender.
5. Season with salt and pepper.
6. Serve hot.

197. Mushroom Barley Soup

A nutritious and flavorful soup that's perfect for a comforting meal.

Servings: 4
Preparation Time: 10 minutes
Cooking Time: 45 minutes
Ingredients:
- 1 pound (450 g) mushrooms, sliced
- 1 onion, chopped
- 2 carrots, sliced
- 2 celery stalks, sliced
- 1/2 cup (100 g) pearl barley
- 4 cups (1 liter) vegetable broth
- 2 tablespoons (30 ml) olive oil
- 2 garlic cloves, minced
- 1 teaspoon (5 g) thyme
- Salt and pepper to taste

Instructions:
1. Heat olive oil in a large pot over medium heat.
2. Add onion, carrots, celery, and garlic, sauté until softened.
3. Add mushrooms and cook until they release their moisture.
4. Stir in barley and vegetable broth, bring to a boil.
5. Reduce heat and simmer for 35-40 minutes until barley is tender.
6. Season with thyme, salt, and pepper.
7. Serve hot.

198. Italian Wedding Soup

A delicious and hearty soup that's perfect for a comforting meal.

Servings: 4
Preparation Time: 15 minutes
Cooking Time: 30 minutes
Ingredients:
- 1/2 pound (225 g) ground turkey
- 1/4 cup (30 g) breadcrumbs
- 1 egg
- 1/4 cup (30 g) grated Parmesan cheese
- 1 onion, chopped
- 2 carrots, sliced
- 2 celery stalks, sliced
- 4 cups (1 liter) chicken broth
- 1 cup (150 g) spinach, chopped
- 1/2 cup (50 g) small pasta
- 2 tablespoons (30 ml) olive oil
- Salt and pepper to taste

Instructions:
1. In a bowl, mix ground turkey, breadcrumbs, egg, and Parmesan cheese.
2. Form small meatballs and set aside.
3. Heat olive oil in a large pot over medium heat.
4. Add onion, carrots, and celery, sauté until softened.
5. Add chicken broth and bring to a boil.
6. Add meatballs and pasta, reduce heat and simmer for 20 minutes.
7. Stir in chopped spinach and cook for an additional 5 minutes.

8. Season with salt and pepper.
9. Serve hot.

199. Cauliflower Soup

A creamy and nutritious soup that's perfect for a healthy meal.

Servings: 4
Preparation Time: 10 minutes
Cooking Time: 30 minutes
Ingredients:

- 1 large head of cauliflower, chopped
- 1 onion, chopped
- 2 garlic cloves, minced
- 4 cups (1 liter) vegetable broth
- 1/2 cup (120 ml) milk
- 2 tablespoons (30 ml) olive oil
- Salt and pepper to taste
- Fresh chives for garnish

Instructions:

1. Heat olive oil in a large pot over medium heat.
2. Add onion and garlic, sauté until softened.
3. Add chopped cauliflower and vegetable broth, bring to a boil.
4. Reduce heat and simmer for 20-25 minutes until cauliflower is tender.
5. Use an immersion blender to blend the soup until smooth.
6. Stir in milk.
7. Season with salt and pepper.
8. Garnish with fresh chives and serve hot.

200. Spicy Sausage Stew

A hearty and flavorful stew that's perfect for a warming meal.

Servings: 4
Preparation Time: 10 minutes
Cooking Time: 40 minutes
Ingredients:

- 1 pound (450 g) spicy sausage, sliced
- 1 onion, chopped
- 2 carrots, sliced
- 2 potatoes, diced
- 1 can (400 g) diced tomatoes
- 4 cups (1 liter) chicken broth
- 2 tablespoons (30 ml) olive oil
- 1 teaspoon (5 g) smoked paprika
- Salt and pepper to taste

Instructions:

1. Heat olive oil in a large pot over medium heat.
2. Add sliced sausage and cook until browned.
3. Add onion, carrots, and potatoes, sauté until softened.
4. Stir in diced tomatoes, chicken broth, and smoked paprika.
5. Bring to a boil, then reduce heat and simmer for 30-35 minutes until vegetables are tender.
6. Season with salt and pepper.
7. Serve hot.

Chapter 16: Nutritious Sides

Side dishes play a crucial role in complementing main courses and ensuring a well-rounded, nutritious meal. They can enhance flavors, add variety, and boost the nutritional value of your plate. This chapter provides a selection of delicious and diabetes-friendly side dishes that are easy to prepare and packed with nutrients.

201. Garlic Roasted Broccoli

A simple and flavorful side dish that's perfect for any meal.

Servings: 4
Preparation Time: 5 minutes
Cooking Time: 20 minutes
Ingredients:

- 1 large head of broccoli, cut into florets
- 2 tablespoons (30 ml) olive oil
- 3 garlic cloves, minced
- Salt and pepper to taste
- Lemon wedges for serving

Instructions:

1. Preheat oven to 425°F (220°C).
2. In a bowl, toss broccoli florets with olive oil, minced garlic, salt, and pepper.
3. Spread broccoli on a baking sheet in a single layer.
4. Roast for 15-20 minutes until the edges are crispy and the broccoli is tender.
5. Serve with lemon wedges.

202. Cauliflower Mash

A creamy and low-carb alternative to mashed potatoes.

Servings: 4
Preparation Time: 10 minutes
Cooking Time: 15 minutes
Ingredients:

- 1 large head of cauliflower, cut into florets
- 2 tablespoons (30 ml) olive oil or butter
- 1/4 cup (60 ml) milk or heavy cream
- 2 garlic cloves, minced
- Salt and pepper to taste
- Fresh chives for garnish

Instructions:

1. Steam or boil cauliflower florets until tender, about 10-15 minutes.
2. Drain and place cauliflower in a food processor.
3. Add olive oil or butter, milk or heavy cream, minced garlic, salt, and pepper.
4. Blend until smooth and creamy.
5. Garnish with fresh chives and serve hot.

203. Balsamic Brussels Sprouts

A delicious and tangy side dish that's perfect for a nutritious meal.

Servings: 4
Preparation Time: 10 minutes
Cooking Time: 20 minutes
Ingredients:

- 1 pound (450 g) Brussels sprouts, halved
- 2 tablespoons (30 ml) balsamic vinegar
- 2 tablespoons (30 ml) olive oil
- 1 tablespoon (15 ml) honey
- Salt and pepper to taste

Instructions:

1. Preheat oven to 425°F (220°C).
2. In a bowl, toss Brussels sprouts with balsamic vinegar, olive oil, honey, salt, and pepper.
3. Spread Brussels sprouts on a baking sheet in a single layer.
4. Roast for 20-25 minutes until caramelized and tender.
5. Serve hot.

204. Quinoa Pilaf

A nutritious and versatile side dish that's perfect for any meal.

Servings: 4
Preparation Time: 10 minutes
Cooking Time: 15 minutes
Ingredients:

- 1 cup (185 g) quinoa, rinsed
- 2 cups (480 ml) vegetable broth
- 1 small onion, chopped
- 1 carrot, diced
- 1 celery stalk, diced
- 2 tablespoons (30 ml) olive oil
- Salt and pepper to taste

Instructions:

1. In a large saucepan, heat olive oil over medium heat.
2. Add onion, carrot, and celery, sauté until softened.
3. Add quinoa and vegetable broth, bring to a boil.
4. Reduce heat, cover, and simmer for 15 minutes until quinoa is cooked and liquid is absorbed.
5. Fluff with a fork, season with salt and pepper, and serve hot.

205. Sweet Potato Fries

A healthy and delicious alternative to regular fries.

Servings: 4
Preparation Time: 10 minutes
Cooking Time: 25 minutes
Ingredients:

- 2 large sweet potatoes, peeled and cut into fries
- 2 tablespoons (30 ml) olive oil
- 1 teaspoon (5 g) paprika
- 1 teaspoon (5 g) garlic powder
- Salt and pepper to taste

Instructions:

1. Preheat oven to 425°F (220°C).

2. In a bowl, toss sweet potato fries with olive oil, paprika, garlic powder, salt, and pepper.
3. Spread fries on a baking sheet in a single layer.
4. Bake for 20-25 minutes, flipping halfway through, until crispy.
5. Serve hot.

206. Green Bean Almondine

A classic and elegant side dish that's perfect for any occasion.

Servings: 4
Preparation Time: 10 minutes
Cooking Time: 10 minutes
Ingredients:

- 1 pound (450 g) green beans, trimmed
- 2 tablespoons (30 g) butter
- 1/4 cup (30 g) sliced almonds
- 1 lemon, zested and juiced
- Salt and pepper to taste

Instructions:

1. Blanch green beans in boiling water for 3-4 minutes, then drain and set aside.
2. In a large skillet, melt butter over medium heat.
3. Add sliced almonds and toast until golden brown.
4. Add green beans, lemon zest, and lemon juice, sauté for 2-3 minutes.
5. Season with salt and pepper and serve hot.

207. Roasted Root Vegetables

A hearty and colorful side dish that's perfect for a nutritious meal.

Servings: 4
Preparation Time: 10 minutes
Cooking Time: 40 minutes
Ingredients:

- 1 large sweet potato, peeled and cubed
- 2 carrots, peeled and sliced
- 2 parsnips, peeled and sliced

- 1 red onion, chopped
- 2 tablespoons (30 ml) olive oil
- 1 teaspoon (5 g) dried rosemary
- Salt and pepper to taste

Instructions:
1. Preheat oven to 425°F (220°C).
2. In a bowl, toss root vegetables with olive oil, dried rosemary, salt, and pepper.
3. Spread vegetables on a baking sheet in a single layer.
4. Roast for 35-40 minutes, stirring occasionally, until tender and caramelized.
5. Serve hot.

208. Zucchini Noodles

A light and refreshing alternative to traditional pasta.

Servings: 4
Preparation Time: 10 minutes
Cooking Time: 5 minutes
Ingredients:
- 4 large zucchinis, spiralized
- 2 tablespoons (30 ml) olive oil
- 2 garlic cloves, minced
- Salt and pepper to taste
- Grated Parmesan cheese for serving

Instructions:
1. Heat olive oil in a large skillet over medium heat.
2. Add minced garlic and sauté until fragrant.
3. Add spiralized zucchinis and cook for 2-3 minutes until just tender.
4. Season with salt and pepper.
5. Serve with grated Parmesan cheese.

209. Spaghetti Squash

A low-carb alternative to pasta that's perfect for a light and healthy side dish.

Servings: 4
Preparation Time: 10 minutes
Cooking Time: 40 minutes

Ingredients:
- 1 large spaghetti squash
- 2 tablespoons (30 ml) olive oil
- Salt and pepper to taste
- Grated Parmesan cheese for serving

Instructions:
1. Preheat oven to 400°F (200°C).
2. Cut spaghetti squash in half lengthwise and remove seeds.
3. Brush the cut sides with olive oil, season with salt and pepper.
4. Place cut-side down on a baking sheet and roast for 35-40 minutes until tender.
5. Use a fork to scrape out the squash into spaghetti-like strands.
6. Serve with grated Parmesan cheese.

210. Lemon Asparagus

A simple and flavorful side dish that's perfect for spring and summer meals.

Servings: 4
Preparation Time: 5 minutes
Cooking Time: 10 minutes
Ingredients:
- 1 pound (450 g) asparagus, trimmed
- 2 tablespoons (30 ml) olive oil
- Juice and zest of 1 lemon
- Salt and pepper to taste

Instructions:
1. Heat olive oil in a large skillet over medium heat.
2. Add asparagus and sauté for 5-7 minutes until tender.
3. Add lemon juice and zest, season with salt and pepper.
4. Serve immediately.

211. Cauliflower Rice

A versatile and low-carb alternative to traditional rice.

Servings: 4
Preparation Time: 10 minutes
Cooking Time: 5 minutes
Ingredients:

- 1 large head of cauliflower, grated or processed into rice-sized pieces
- 2 tablespoons (30 ml) olive oil
- 1 garlic clove, minced
- Salt and pepper to taste
- Fresh parsley for garnish

Instructions:

1. Heat olive oil in a large skillet over medium heat.
2. Add minced garlic and sauté until fragrant.
3. Add cauliflower rice and cook for 3-5 minutes until tender.
4. Season with salt and pepper.
5. Garnish with fresh parsley and serve hot.

212. Wilted Spinach

A quick and nutritious side dish that's perfect for any meal.

Servings: 4
Preparation Time: 5 minutes
Cooking Time: 5 minutes
Ingredients:

- 1 pound (450 g) fresh spinach, washed and trimmed
- 2 tablespoons (30 ml) olive oil
- 2 garlic cloves, minced
- Salt and pepper to taste

Instructions:

1. Heat olive oil in a large skillet over medium heat.
2. Add minced garlic and sauté until fragrant.
3. Add spinach and cook, stirring constantly, until wilted.
4. Season with salt and pepper.

5. Serve immediately.

213. Grilled Veggie Platter

A colorful and nutritious side dish that's perfect for grilling season.

Servings: 4
Preparation Time: 10 minutes
Cooking Time: 10 minutes
Ingredients:

- 1 zucchini, sliced
- 1 yellow squash, sliced
- 1 red bell pepper, sliced
- 1 red onion, sliced
- 2 tablespoons (30 ml) olive oil
- Salt and pepper to taste
- Fresh basil for garnish

Instructions:

1. Preheat grill to medium-high heat.
2. In a bowl, toss vegetables with olive oil, salt, and pepper.
3. Grill vegetables for 8-10 minutes until tender and slightly charred.
4. Garnish with fresh basil and serve hot.

214. Baked Sweet Potatoes

A sweet and nutritious side dish that's perfect for any meal.

Servings: 4
Preparation Time: 5 minutes
Cooking Time: 45 minutes
Ingredients:

- 4 medium sweet potatoes
- 2 tablespoons (30 ml) olive oil
- Salt and pepper to taste

Instructions:

1. Preheat oven to 400°F (200°C).
2. Wash sweet potatoes and pierce each several times with a fork.
3. Rub with olive oil and season with salt and pepper.
4. Place on a baking sheet and bake for 40-45 minutes until tender.
5. Serve hot.

215. Steamed Artichokes

A unique and healthy side dish that's perfect for a special meal.

Servings: 4
Preparation Time: 10 minutes
Cooking Time: 30 minutes
Ingredients:

- 4 large artichokes
- 1 lemon, halved
- 2 garlic cloves, sliced
- Salt to taste

Instructions:

1. Trim the artichokes, removing the tough outer leaves and cutting off the top third.
2. Rub the cut parts with lemon to prevent browning.
3. Fill a large pot with 1 inch of water, add garlic slices and lemon halves.
4. Place a steamer basket in the pot and bring water to a boil.
5. Add artichokes, cover, and steam for 25-30 minutes until tender.
6. Serve hot or at room temperature.

216. Roasted Beet Salad

A vibrant and nutritious salad that's perfect for any meal.

Servings: 4
Preparation Time: 10 minutes
Cooking Time: 45 minutes
Ingredients:

- 4 medium beets, peeled and cut into wedges
- 2 tablespoons (30 ml) olive oil
- Salt and pepper to taste
- 4 cups (120 g) mixed greens
- 1/4 cup (30 g) goat cheese, crumbled
- 1/4 cup (30 g) walnuts, toasted
- 2 tablespoons (30 ml) balsamic vinaigrette

Instructions:

1. Preheat oven to 400°F (200°C).
2. Toss beet wedges with olive oil, salt, and pepper.
3. Spread on a baking sheet and roast for 40-45 minutes until tender.
4. In a large bowl, combine mixed greens, roasted beets, goat cheese, and walnuts.
5. Drizzle with balsamic vinaigrette and toss to combine.
6. Serve immediately.

217. Stuffed Portobello Mushrooms

A hearty and flavorful side dish that's perfect for any occasion.

Servings: 4
Preparation Time: 15 minutes
Cooking Time: 20 minutes
Ingredients:

- 4 large Portobello mushrooms, stems removed
- 1 cup (150 g) spinach, chopped
- 1/2 cup (50 g) shredded mozzarella cheese
- 1/4 cup (30 g) grated Parmesan cheese
- 2 garlic cloves, minced
- 2 tablespoons (30 ml) olive oil
- Salt and pepper to taste

Instructions:

1. Preheat oven to 375°F (190°C).
2. Heat olive oil in a skillet over medium heat.
3. Add garlic and spinach, sauté until wilted.
4. Remove from heat and stir in mozzarella and Parmesan cheese.
5. Stuff each mushroom cap with the spinach mixture.
6. Place mushrooms on a baking sheet and bake for 15-20 minutes until the cheese is melted and bubbly.
7. Serve hot.

218. Sautéed Kale with Garlic

A quick and nutritious side dish that's packed with flavor.

Servings: 4
Preparation Time: 5 minutes
Cooking Time: 10 minutes
Ingredients:

- 1 pound (450 g) kale, washed and chopped
- 2 tablespoons (30 ml) olive oil
- 3 garlic cloves, minced
- Salt and pepper to taste
- Lemon wedges for serving

Instructions:

1. Heat olive oil in a large skillet over medium heat.
2. Add garlic and sauté until fragrant.
3. Add chopped kale and cook, stirring constantly, until wilted, about 5-7 minutes.
4. Season with salt and pepper.
5. Serve with lemon wedges.

219. Parsnip Mash

A creamy and nutritious alternative to traditional mashed potatoes.

Servings: 4
Preparation Time: 10 minutes
Cooking Time: 20 minutes
Ingredients:

- 1 pound (450 g) parsnips, peeled and chopped
- 2 tablespoons (30 g) butter
- 1/4 cup (60 ml) milk or heavy cream
- Salt and pepper to taste
- Fresh chives for garnish

Instructions:

1. Boil parsnips in a large pot of water until tender, about 15-20 minutes.
2. Drain and transfer parsnips to a bowl.
3. Add butter and milk or heavy cream.
4. Mash until smooth and creamy.
5. Season with salt and pepper.
6. Garnish with fresh chives and serve hot.

220. Cabbage Steaks

A simple and flavorful side dish that's perfect for any meal.

Servings: 4
Preparation Time: 10 minutes
Cooking Time: 30 minutes
Ingredients:

- 1 large head of cabbage, sliced into 1-inch steaks
- 2 tablespoons (30 ml) olive oil
- 1 teaspoon (5 g) garlic powder
- Salt and pepper to taste
- Fresh parsley for garnish

Instructions:

1. Preheat oven to 400°F (200°C).
2. Brush cabbage steaks with olive oil and season with garlic powder, salt, and pepper.
3. Place cabbage steaks on a baking sheet and roast for 25-30 minutes until tender and edges are crispy.
4. Garnish with fresh parsley and serve hot.

Extra Chapter: Diabetic Air Fryer Recipes

Air fryers are fantastic tools for preparing healthy meals with less oil, making them ideal for diabetes management. This chapter provides a variety of delicious and diabetes-friendly air fryer recipes that are quick, easy, and packed with flavor.

221. Air Fryer Chicken Tenders
A healthy and crispy alternative to traditional fried chicken.
Servings: 4
Preparation Time: 10 minutes
Cooking Time: 15 minutes
Ingredients:
- 1 pound (450 g) chicken tenders
- 1 cup (100 g) almond flour
- 1 teaspoon (5 g) paprika
- 1 teaspoon (5 g) garlic powder
- 1/2 teaspoon (2.5 g) salt
- 1/2 teaspoon (2.5 g) black pepper
- 2 eggs, beaten

Instructions:
1. Preheat air fryer to 400°F (200°C).
2. In a bowl, mix almond flour, paprika, garlic powder, salt, and pepper.
3. Dip each chicken tender into the beaten eggs, then coat with the almond flour mixture.
4. Place tenders in a single layer in the air fryer basket.
5. Cook for 10-15 minutes, turning halfway through, until golden and cooked through.
6. Serve hot.

222. Air Fryer Zucchini Chips
A crunchy and healthy snack that's perfect for any time of the day.
Servings: 4
Preparation Time: 10 minutes
Cooking Time: 15 minutes
Ingredients:
- 2 medium zucchinis, sliced thinly
- 1/2 cup (50 g) almond flour
- 1/4 cup (25 g) grated Parmesan cheese
- 1 teaspoon (5 g) garlic powder
- 1 teaspoon (5 g) Italian seasoning
- Salt and pepper to taste
- Olive oil spray

Instructions:
1. Preheat air fryer to 375°F (190°C).
2. In a bowl, mix almond flour, Parmesan cheese, garlic powder, Italian seasoning, salt, and pepper.
3. Dip zucchini slices into the mixture, coating evenly.
4. Place zucchini slices in a single layer in the air fryer basket and spray with olive oil.
5. Cook for 10-15 minutes, turning halfway through, until crispy.
6. Serve immediately.

223. Air Fryer Salmon
A quick and healthy way to enjoy perfectly cooked salmon.
Servings: 4
Preparation Time: 5 minutes
Cooking Time: 10 minutes
Ingredients:
- 4 salmon fillets
- 2 tablespoons (30 ml) olive oil
- 1 teaspoon (5 g) garlic powder
- 1 teaspoon (5 g) paprika
- Salt and pepper to taste
- Lemon wedges for serving

Instructions:
1. Preheat air fryer to 400°F (200°C).
2. Brush salmon fillets with olive oil and season with garlic powder, paprika, salt, and pepper.

3. Place salmon fillets in the air fryer basket.
4. Cook for 8-10 minutes until the salmon is cooked through and flakes easily with a fork.
5. Serve with lemon wedges.

224. Air Fryer Brussels Sprouts

Crispy and flavorful Brussels sprouts that make a perfect side dish.

Servings: 4
Preparation Time: 5 minutes
Cooking Time: 12 minutes
Ingredients:

- 1 pound (450 g) Brussels sprouts, halved
- 2 tablespoons (30 ml) olive oil
- 1 teaspoon (5 g) garlic powder
- Salt and pepper to taste
- Balsamic glaze for serving (optional)

Instructions:

1. Preheat air fryer to 375°F (190°C).
2. In a bowl, toss Brussels sprouts with olive oil, garlic powder, salt, and pepper.
3. Place Brussels sprouts in the air fryer basket in a single layer.
4. Cook for 12-15 minutes, shaking the basket halfway through, until crispy and browned.
5. Drizzle with balsamic glaze if desired and serve hot.

225. Air Fryer Cauliflower Bites

A tasty and healthy snack that's perfect for any occasion.

Servings: 4
Preparation Time: 10 minutes
Cooking Time: 15 minutes
Ingredients:

- 1 head of cauliflower, cut into florets
- 1/2 cup (60 g) almond flour
- 2 eggs, beaten
- 1 teaspoon (5 g) paprika
- 1 teaspoon (5 g) garlic powder
- Salt and pepper to taste

- Olive oil spray

Instructions:

1. Preheat air fryer to 400°F (200°C).
2. In a bowl, mix almond flour, paprika, garlic powder, salt, and pepper.
3. Dip cauliflower florets into the beaten eggs, then coat with the almond flour mixture.
4. Place cauliflower in a single layer in the air fryer basket and spray with olive oil.
5. Cook for 15 minutes, shaking the basket halfway through, until golden and crispy.
6. Serve immediately.

226. Air Fryer Chicken Wings

Delicious and crispy chicken wings without the extra oil.

Servings: 4
Preparation Time: 10 minutes
Cooking Time: 25 minutes
Ingredients:

- 1 pound (450 g) chicken wings
- 1 tablespoon (15 ml) olive oil
- 1 teaspoon (5 g) garlic powder
- 1 teaspoon (5 g) paprika
- 1 teaspoon (5 g) salt
- 1/2 teaspoon (2.5 g) black pepper
- Hot sauce for serving (optional)

Instructions:

1. Preheat air fryer to 400°F (200°C).
2. In a bowl, toss chicken wings with olive oil, garlic powder, paprika, salt, and pepper.
3. Place wings in the air fryer basket in a single layer.
4. Cook for 20-25 minutes, shaking the basket halfway through, until crispy and cooked through.
5. Serve with hot sauce if desired.

227. Air Fryer Tofu Bites

A crispy and delicious plant-based snack or side dish.

Servings: 4
Preparation Time: 10 minutes
Cooking Time: 15 minutes
Ingredients:

- 1 block of firm tofu, pressed and cubed
- 2 tablespoons (30 ml) soy sauce
- 1 tablespoon (15 ml) sesame oil
- 1 teaspoon (5 g) garlic powder
- 1 teaspoon (5 g) onion powder
- 1 tablespoon (15 ml) cornstarch

Instructions:

1. Preheat air fryer to 375°F (190°C).
2. In a bowl, toss tofu cubes with soy sauce, sesame oil, garlic powder, and onion powder.
3. Sprinkle cornstarch over tofu and toss to coat evenly.
4. Place tofu in a single layer in the air fryer basket.
5. Cook for 12-15 minutes, shaking the basket halfway through, until crispy.
6. Serve hot.

228. Air Fryer Stuffed Peppers

A healthy and satisfying dish that's perfect for a main course or side.

Servings: 4
Preparation Time: 15 minutes
Cooking Time: 15 minutes
Ingredients:

- 4 bell peppers, tops cut off and seeds removed
- 1 cup (185 g) cooked quinoa
- 1/2 cup (75 g) black beans, rinsed and drained
- 1/2 cup (75 g) corn kernels
- 1/4 cup (30 g) shredded cheese
- 1 teaspoon (5 g) cumin
- Salt and pepper to taste

Instructions:

1. Preheat air fryer to 375°F (190°C).
2. In a bowl, mix cooked quinoa, black beans, corn, cheese, cumin, salt, and pepper.
3. Stuff each bell pepper with the quinoa mixture.
4. Place stuffed peppers in the air fryer basket.
5. Cook for 12-15 minutes until the peppers are tender and the filling is heated through.
6. Serve hot.

229. Air Fryer Carrot Fries

A sweet and savory alternative to traditional fries.

Servings: 4
Preparation Time: 5 minutes
Cooking Time: 15 minutes
Ingredients:

- 4 large carrots, peeled and cut into fries
- 2 tablespoons (30 ml) olive oil
- 1 teaspoon (5 g) garlic powder
- 1 teaspoon (5 g) paprika
- Salt and pepper to taste

Instructions:

1. Preheat air fryer to 400°F (200°C).
2. In a bowl, toss carrot fries with olive oil, garlic powder, paprika, salt, and pepper.
3. Place carrot fries in a single layer in the air fryer basket.
4. Cook for 12-15 minutes, shaking the basket halfway through, until crispy and tender.
5. Serve hot.

230. Air Fryer Shrimp

A quick and healthy way to enjoy perfectly cooked shrimp.

Servings: 4
Preparation Time: 10 minutes
Cooking Time: 8 minutes

Ingredients:
- 1 pound (450 g) large shrimp, peeled and deveined
- 2 tablespoons (30 ml) olive oil
- 1 teaspoon (5 g) garlic powder
- 1 teaspoon (5 g) paprika
- Salt and pepper to taste
- Lemon wedges for serving

Instructions:
1. Preheat air fryer to 400°F (200°C).
2. In a bowl, toss shrimp with olive oil, garlic powder, paprika, salt, and pepper.
3. Place shrimp in the air fryer basket in a single layer.
4. Cook for 6-8 minutes until shrimp are pink and cooked through.
5. Serve with lemon wedges.

231. Air Fryer Asparagus

A simple and nutritious side dish that's perfect for any meal.

Servings: 4
Preparation Time: 5 minutes
Cooking Time: 10 minutes
Ingredients:
- 1 pound (450 g) asparagus, trimmed
- 2 tablespoons (30 ml) olive oil
- 1 teaspoon (5 g) garlic powder
- Salt and pepper to taste

Instructions:
1. Preheat air fryer to 400°F (200°C).
2. In a bowl, toss asparagus with olive oil, garlic powder, salt, and pepper.
3. Place asparagus in the air fryer basket in a single layer.
4. Cook for 8-10 minutes until tender and slightly crispy.
5. Serve hot.

232. Air Fryer Meatballs

A healthy and flavorful option for a protein-packed meal.

Servings: 4
Preparation Time: 15 minutes
Cooking Time: 12 minutes
Ingredients:
- 1 pound (450 g) ground turkey or chicken
- 1/4 cup (30 g) breadcrumbs
- 1 egg
- 1/4 cup (30 g) grated Parmesan cheese
- 2 garlic cloves, minced
- 1 teaspoon (5 g) Italian seasoning
- Salt and pepper to taste

Instructions:
1. Preheat air fryer to 375°F (190°C).
2. In a bowl, mix ground meat, breadcrumbs, egg, Parmesan cheese, garlic, Italian seasoning, salt, and pepper.
3. Form the mixture into meatballs and place them in the air fryer basket in a single layer.
4. Cook for 10-12 minutes until cooked through and golden brown.
5. Serve hot.

233. Air Fryer Eggplant Parmesan

A healthier take on a classic Italian dish.

Servings: 4
Preparation Time: 15 minutes
Cooking Time: 15 minutes
Ingredients:
- 1 large eggplant, sliced
- 1 cup (100 g) almond flour
- 1/2 cup (50 g) grated Parmesan cheese
- 1 teaspoon (5 g) Italian seasoning
- 2 eggs, beaten
- 1 cup (240 ml) marinara sauce
- 1 cup (100 g) shredded mozzarella cheese
- Olive oil spray

Instructions:
1. Preheat air fryer to 375°F (190°C).
2. In a bowl, mix almond flour, Parmesan cheese, and Italian seasoning.

3. Dip eggplant slices into the beaten eggs, then coat with the almond flour mixture.
4. Place eggplant slices in the air fryer basket and spray with olive oil.
5. Cook for 10-12 minutes until golden and crispy.
6. Top with marinara sauce and mozzarella cheese, cook for an additional 3 minutes until cheese is melted.
7. Serve hot.

234. Air Fryer Green Beans

A quick and easy side dish that's full of flavor.
Servings: 4
Preparation Time: 5 minutes
Cooking Time: 10 minutes
Ingredients:

- 1 pound (450 g) green beans, trimmed
- 2 tablespoons (30 ml) olive oil
- 1 teaspoon (5 g) garlic powder
- Salt and pepper to taste
- Lemon wedges for serving

Instructions:

1. Preheat air fryer to 375°F (190°C).
2. In a bowl, toss green beans with olive oil, garlic powder, salt, and pepper.
3. Place green beans in the air fryer basket in a single layer.
4. Cook for 8-10 minutes until tender and slightly crispy.
5. Serve with lemon wedges.

235. Air Fryer Apple Chips

A sweet and healthy snack that's perfect for any time of day.
Servings: 4
Preparation Time: 5 minutes
Cooking Time: 20 minutes
Ingredients:

- 2 large apples, thinly sliced
- 1 teaspoon (5 g) ground cinnamon

Instructions:

1. Preheat air fryer to 300°F (150°C).
2. In a bowl, toss apple slices with ground cinnamon.
3. Place apple slices in a single layer in the air fryer basket.
4. Cook for 15-20 minutes, turning halfway through, until crispy.
5. Serve immediately or store in an airtight container.

60 Days Meal Plan

	Breakfast	Lunch	Snack	Dinner
Day 1	Smoothie Bowls	Veggie Stir-Fry	Garlic Roasted Broccoli	Sautéed Clams
Day 2	Stuffed Bell Peppers	Grilled Veggie Skewers	Guacamole and Veggie Dippers	Veggie Burger
Day 3	Chia Seed Pudding	Baked Chicken Breast	Lemon Asparagus	Chicken and Veggie Stir-Fry
Day 4	Air Fryer Stuffed Peppers	Quinoa and Black Bean Bowl	Balsamic Brussels Sprouts	Garlic Parmesan Crusted Salmon
Day 5	Almond Flour Brownies	Grilled Turkey Burgers	Fresh Fruit Salad	Clam Chowder
Day 6	Muesli Mix	Black Bean Tacos	Split Pea Soup	Baked Salmon with Asparagus
Day 7	Quinoa Salad	Chickpea and Kale Soup	Quinoa Pilaf	Fish and Veggie Foil Packs
Day 8	Berry Chia Pudding	Eggplant Parmesan	Almond Flour Crackers	Mussels in White Wine Sauce
Day 9	Greek Yogurt Parfait with Berries	Chicken Stir-Fry	Sweet Potato Fries	Beef and Broccoli
Day 10	Pumpkin Spice Muffins	Lemon Garlic Chicken	Hard-Boiled Eggs	Lentil Soup
Day 11	Chocolate Chia Pudding	Tuna Salad Lettuce Wraps	Green Bean Almondine	Zucchini Lasagna
Day 12	Cottage Cheese with Fresh Fruit	Ceviche	Popcorn	Shrimp Scampi
Day 13	Peanut Butter Bliss Balls	Grilled Chicken Salad	Roasted Root Vegetables	Stuffed Bell Peppers
Day 14	Carrot Cake Bites	Turkey Meatloaf	Grilled Veggie Platter	Baked Halibut
Day 15	Veggie Omelette	Roasted Veggie Wrap	Smoked Salmon on Cucumber Slices	Spinach and Feta Stuffed Mushrooms
Day 16	Zucchini Bread	Chicken Parmesan	Steamed Artichokes	Lobster Tail with Garlic Butter
Day 17	Whole Grain Avocado Toast	Lentil Soup	Stuffed Portobello Mushrooms	Pan-Seared Trout
Day 18	Banana Nut Bread	Stuffed Chicken Breast	Baked Sweet Potatoes	Pork Tenderloin with Brussels Sprouts

	Breakfast	Lunch	Snack	Dinner
Day 19	Guacamole Deviled Eggs	Zucchini Noodles	Air Fryer Zucchini Chips	Cauliflower Steak
Day 20	Mini Quiches	Turkey and Avocado Wrap	Roasted Beet Salad	Salmon Patties
Day 21	Quinoa Breakfast Bowl	BBQ Chicken Skewers	Air Fryer Brussels Sprouts	Quinoa-Stuffed Squash
Day 22	Veggie Spring Rolls	Chicken Fajitas	Berry and Nut Mix	Chickpea Curry
Day 23	Spiced Apple Compote	Cauliflower Rice Salad	Dark Chocolate Squares	Ratatouille
Day 24	Scrambled Tofu	Roasted Butternut Squash	Coconut Flour Cookies	Grilled Mahi-Mahi
Day 25	Bruschetta with Tomato and Basil	Thai Chicken Salad	Cabbage Steaks	Stuffed Zucchini Boats
Day 26	Carrot Cake Bites	Roasted Turkey Breast	Air Fryer Tofu Bites	Lemon Garlic Shrimp
Day 27	Almond Flour Pancakes	Spinach and Strawberry Salad	Sugar-Free Cheesecake	Veggie Pizza
Day 28	Smoked Salmon Roll-Ups	Chicken Curry	Celery with Peanut Butter	Lentil and Veggie Stew
Day 29	Breakfast Burritos	Spaghetti Squash	Crab Cakes	Turkey Meatballs with Spaghetti Squash
Day 30	Cheese Stuffed Peppers	Greek Lemon Chicken	Edamame	Sweet Potato and Black Bean Chili
Day 31	Muesli Mix	Zucchini Noodles with Pesto	Air Fryer Eggplant Parmesan	Baked Cod with Lemon
Day 32	Overnight Oats	Honey Mustard Chicken	Protein Balls	Mushroom Stroganoff
Day 33	Stuffed Bell Peppers	Air Fryer Salmon	Dark Chocolate Avocado Mousse	Grilled Veggie Skewers
Day 34	Chia Seed Pudding	Sweet Potato and Black Bean Chili	Apple Cinnamon Crisp	Veggie Shepherd's Pie
Day 35	Cheese and Whole Grain Crackers	Spicy Chicken Wings	Greek Yogurt with Nuts	Eggplant Parmesan
Day 36	Berry Breakfast Muffins	Mediterranean Bowl	Air Fryer Cauliflower Bites	Spinach and Ricotta Stuffed Shells
Day 37	Chocolate Chia Pudding	Chicken Tacos	Lemon Blueberry Bars	Cauliflower Crust Pizza
Day 38	Cottage Cheese with Fresh Fruit	Eggplant Roll-Ups	Veggie Chips	Grilled Portobello Mushrooms

	Breakfast	Lunch	Snack	Dinner
Day 39	Peanut Butter Bliss Balls	Herb-Crusted Chicken	Vanilla Bean Panna Cotta	Tuna Steaks with Mango Salsa
Day 40	Spinach and Feta Frittata	Chicken and Veggie Kebabs	Keto Chocolate Cake	Beef and Vegetable Soup
Day 41	Zucchini Bread	Shrimp and Avocado Salad	Roasted Chickpeas	Chicken Fajita Bowl
Day 42	Spiced Apple Compote	Chicken Noodle Soup	Mango Sorbet	Tomato Basil Soup
Day 43	Veggie Omelette	Teriyaki Chicken	Apple Slices with Almond Butter	Shrimp and Veggie Skewers
Day 44	Nut Butter and Banana Wrap	Air Fryer Chicken Tenders	Raspberry Almond Tart	Baked Cod with Green Beans
Day 45	Air Fryer Stuffed Peppers	Broccoli and Cheese Soup	Air Fryer Green Beans	Turkey Chili
Day 46	Egg Muffins	Air Fryer Meatballs	Air Fryer Carrot Fries	Fish Tacos with Slaw
Day 47	Quinoa Salad	Buffalo Chicken Lettuce Wraps	Strawberry Shortcake	Seared Scallops with Garlic Butter
Day 48	Berry Chia Pudding	Falafel Wrap	Hummus and Veggie Sticks	Broccoli Cheddar Soup
Day 49	Savory Oatmeal	Balsamic Glazed Chicken	Lemon Yogurt Cake	Grilled Chicken with Avocado Salsa
Day 50	Mini Quiches	Butternut Squash Soup	Cheese and Whole Grain Crackers	Chicken Tortilla Soup
Day 51	Quinoa Breakfast Bowl	Spaghetti Squash Bowl	Coconut Macaroons	Baked Tilapia with Herbs
Day 52	Veggie Spring Rolls	Meat and Cheese Platter	Air Fryer Asparagus	Herb-Crusted Tilapia
Day 53	Buckwheat Pancakes	Chicken Satay	Cottage Cheese and Pineapple	Minestrone Soup
Day 54	Cauliflower Rice Salad	Spicy Tuna Tartare	Caprese Skewers	Thai Red Curry
Day 55	Roasted Butternut Squash	Greek Salad with Grilled Fish	Berry and Nut Mix	Vegetable Stew
Day 56	Thai Chicken Salad	Baked Chicken Breast	Cucumber Bites	Beef Stir-Fry with Snow Peas
Day 57	Breakfast Salad	Air Fryer Chicken Wings	Mixed Nuts and Seeds	Clam Chowder

	Breakfast	**Lunch**	**Snack**	**Dinner**
Day 58	Smoothie Bowls	Lemon Garlic Chicken	Shrimp Cocktail	Lemon Butter Shrimp
Day 59	Stuffed Bell Peppers	Spicy Chicken Wings	Air Fryer Apple Chips	Stuffed Zucchini Boats
Day 60	Chia Seed Pudding	Air Fryer Shrimp	Avocado and Tomato Slices	Grilled Salmon with Avocado Salsa

Conclusion

Reflecting on Your Journey

As you reach the end of this cookbook, take a moment to reflect on the incredible journey you've embarked upon. Managing type 2 diabetes is not merely about restricting your diet; it's about embracing a new lifestyle that prioritizes your health and well-being. The recipes and information provided here are designed to empower you to make healthier choices without sacrificing flavor and enjoyment in your meals.

Think back to when you first began. Perhaps you felt overwhelmed by the diagnosis or unsure about how to adjust your eating habits. Now, you've armed yourself with knowledge about diabetes, from understanding the basics of the condition to learning how diet and lifestyle changes can make a significant impact. You've explored a variety of delicious, diabetes-friendly recipes that demonstrate healthy eating doesn't have to be boring or bland.

Maintaining Long-term Healthy Habits

Sustaining the healthy habits you've learned is crucial for long-term diabetes management. Consistency is key, and small, daily choices add up over time. Here are some tips to help you maintain these habits:

1. **Plan Your Meals:** Meal planning can save you time, reduce stress, and ensure you're eating balanced meals. Use the 60-day meal plan provided in this book as a starting point, and feel free to customize it according to your preferences and seasonal availability of ingredients.

2. **Stay Active:** Incorporate regular physical activity into your routine. Exercise helps regulate blood sugar levels, improves your mood, and boosts overall health. Find activities you enjoy, whether it's walking, swimming, dancing, or yoga, and aim for at least 30 minutes a day.

3. **Monitor Your Health:** Keep track of your blood sugar levels, weight, and overall health. Regular check-ups with your healthcare provider are essential to monitor your progress and make any necessary adjustments to your management plan.

4. **Stay Hydrated:** Drinking plenty of water is important for everyone, especially for managing diabetes. Aim for at least eight glasses of water a day to help maintain proper hydration and support your body's functions.

5. **Mindful Eating:** Pay attention to your hunger and fullness cues, and avoid mindless snacking. Eating mindfully can help you enjoy your food more and prevent overeating.

Tips for Staying Motivated

Staying motivated can be challenging, especially when life gets busy or stressful. Here are some strategies to keep your motivation high:

1. **Set Realistic Goals:** Setting achievable goals gives you something to work towards and can provide a sense of accomplishment. Whether it's trying a new recipe each week or hitting a certain number of steps each day, small goals can lead to big changes.

2. **Find Support:** Surround yourself with a supportive community. This could be family, friends, or a diabetes support group. Sharing your journey with others can provide encouragement, accountability, and inspiration.

3. **Celebrate Milestones:** Recognize and celebrate your achievements, no matter how small they may seem. Whether it's maintaining your blood sugar levels within target range or trying a new vegetable, each step forward is worth celebrating.

4. **Stay Informed:** Keep learning about diabetes and nutrition. New research and recipes are constantly emerging, and staying informed can keep your journey fresh and exciting.

5. **Be Kind to Yourself:** Understand that setbacks are a normal part of any journey. If you have a bad day, don't dwell on it. Instead, focus on getting back on track the next day. Self-compassion is crucial for long-term success.

Final Encouragement and Inspiration

You've come a long way, and your dedication to managing your diabetes is truly commendable. The journey towards better health is ongoing, and it's important to recognize that each choice you make is a step in the right direction. Remember, you're not alone in this journey. There's a community of people, resources, and support systems ready to help you succeed.

As you continue to experiment with the recipes and techniques in this book, I encourage you to get creative in the kitchen. Don't be afraid to try new ingredients, modify recipes to suit your tastes, and explore different cuisines. Cooking is an art, and it's a wonderful way to nurture your body and soul.

Reflect on Your Accomplishments

Finally, take a moment to reflect on how far you've come. Managing diabetes is a significant undertaking, and every step you take towards better health is a victory. Whether it's preparing a homemade meal, choosing a healthy snack, or engaging in regular exercise, these actions contribute to your overall well-being.

Remember, this journey is about progress, not perfection. Celebrate your successes, learn from your challenges, and continue to move forward with confidence and determination. You have the tools, knowledge, and support to thrive, and your commitment to a healthier lifestyle is an inspiration.

Thank you for allowing this book to be a part of your journey. May it continue to serve as a resource, a guide, and a source of inspiration as you navigate your path to better health and happiness. Keep cooking, keep learning, and most importantly, keep believing in yourself. Your journey is unique, and every healthy choice you make is a testament to your strength and resilience.

With heartfelt encouragement and best wishes for your continued success.

Manufactured by Amazon.ca
Acheson, AB

16396152R00066